Alphabet Tracing COLOR BY & LETTERS

PreK workbook

A Fun Practice Workbook for Pre-K

Mare Robbins

YOUNG
SCHOLAR BOOKS

Copyright © 2023 by Young Scholar Books, New Jersey

Published in the United States by Young Scholar Books,
an imprint of Ciparum LLC, New Jersey

All rights reserved. No part of this publication may be reproduced, stored in a retrieval system, or transmitted, in any form or by any means, electronic, mechanical, photocopying, recording, or otherwise, without prior written permission from the publisher. Requests to the publisher should be addressed to Ciparum LLC, 270 Sparta Ave., Suite 104, PMB 152, Sparta, NJ 07871.

Interior and cover design: Mare Robbins
Images used under license from Canva and Depositphotos.com

ISBN: 978-1-63589-818-7

NOTE TO PARENTS AND TEACHERS

Greetings from Mare Robbins! Unleash the wonder of learning in your young ones with our new alphabet tracing and color-by-letters activity workbook—an invigorating voyage into the world of letters. We firmly believe that early literacy skills pave the way to a future of endless possibilities.

Our meticulously crafted workbook is more than just an alphabet primer—it's a ticket to an interactive learning journey where children can trace, write, color, and discover. Your little learner will not only get familiar with both uppercase and lowercase alphabets but will also embark on an exciting adventure of unmasking vibrant images hidden within letters.

Our activity book has been designed to cater to your child's innate curiosity and creativity while fostering crucial motor skills. They'll find themselves immersed in a world of colors and shapes that will stimulate their hand-eye coordination, pencil control and refine their dexterity.

In true learning-by-doing spirit, the book invites continuous practice, a proven way to achieve mastery. Your child's journey through these pages, armed with just a pencil and crayons, will be further enriched by the indispensable support of a parent, teacher, caregiver, or even an older sibling.

Our workbook is more than a learning tool—it's a confidence builder. Each completed activity paves the way for a new achievement, instilling a sense of accomplishment in your child. With ample opportunities to practice and perfect, your child will not only master handwriting but will also foster a love for learning.

We believe this book is just the beginning of an enlightening journey. If you and your child enjoyed this magical learning experience, we would appreciate a review on any platform where this book is sold. Your words of appreciation will inspire us to create even more exciting learning materials for our young explorers. Grab a copy today and have your child PreK ready.

Thanks,
Mare Robbins.

HANDWRITING PRE-PRACTICE

HANDWRITING PRE-PRACTICE

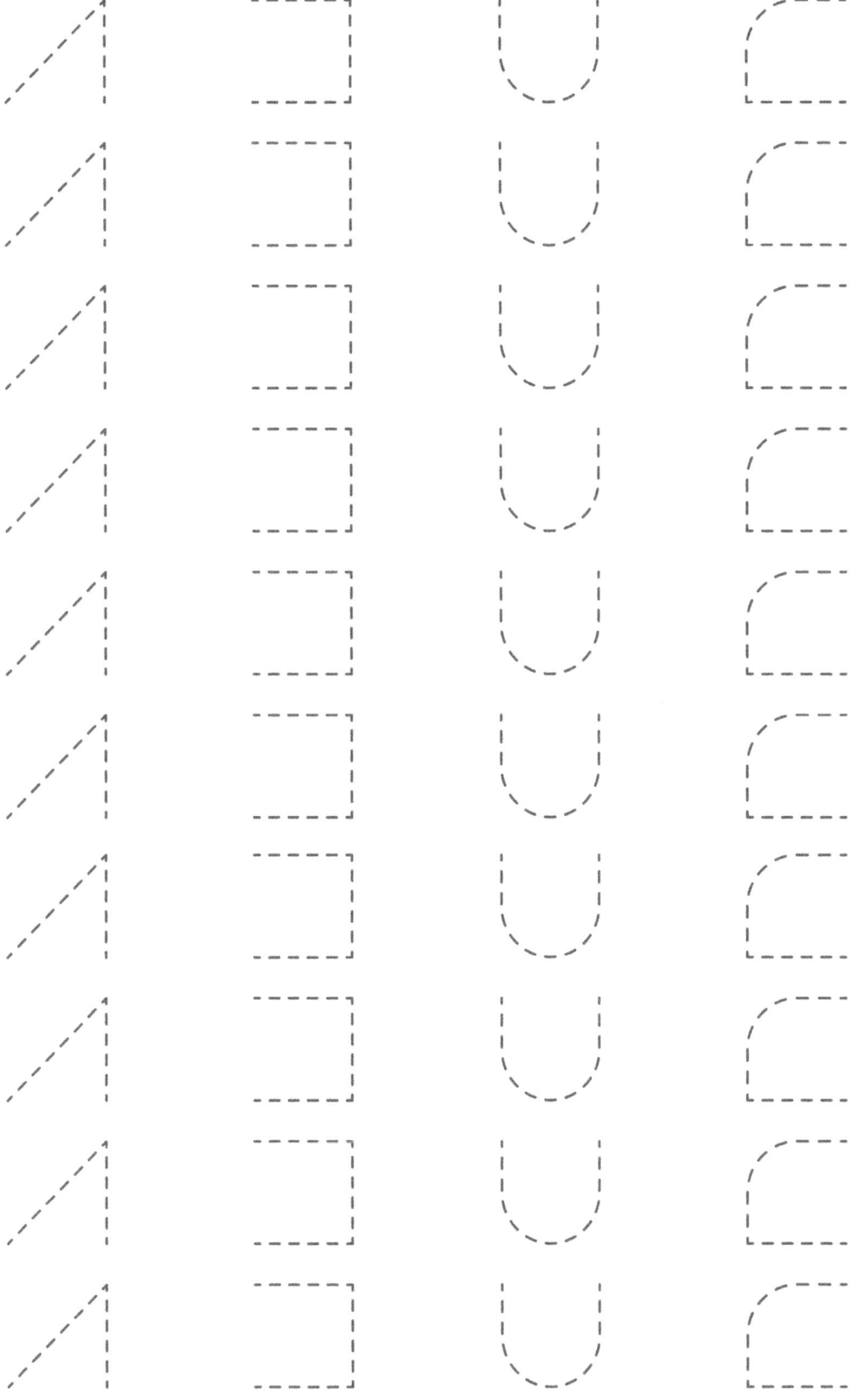

HANDWRITING PRE-PRACTICE

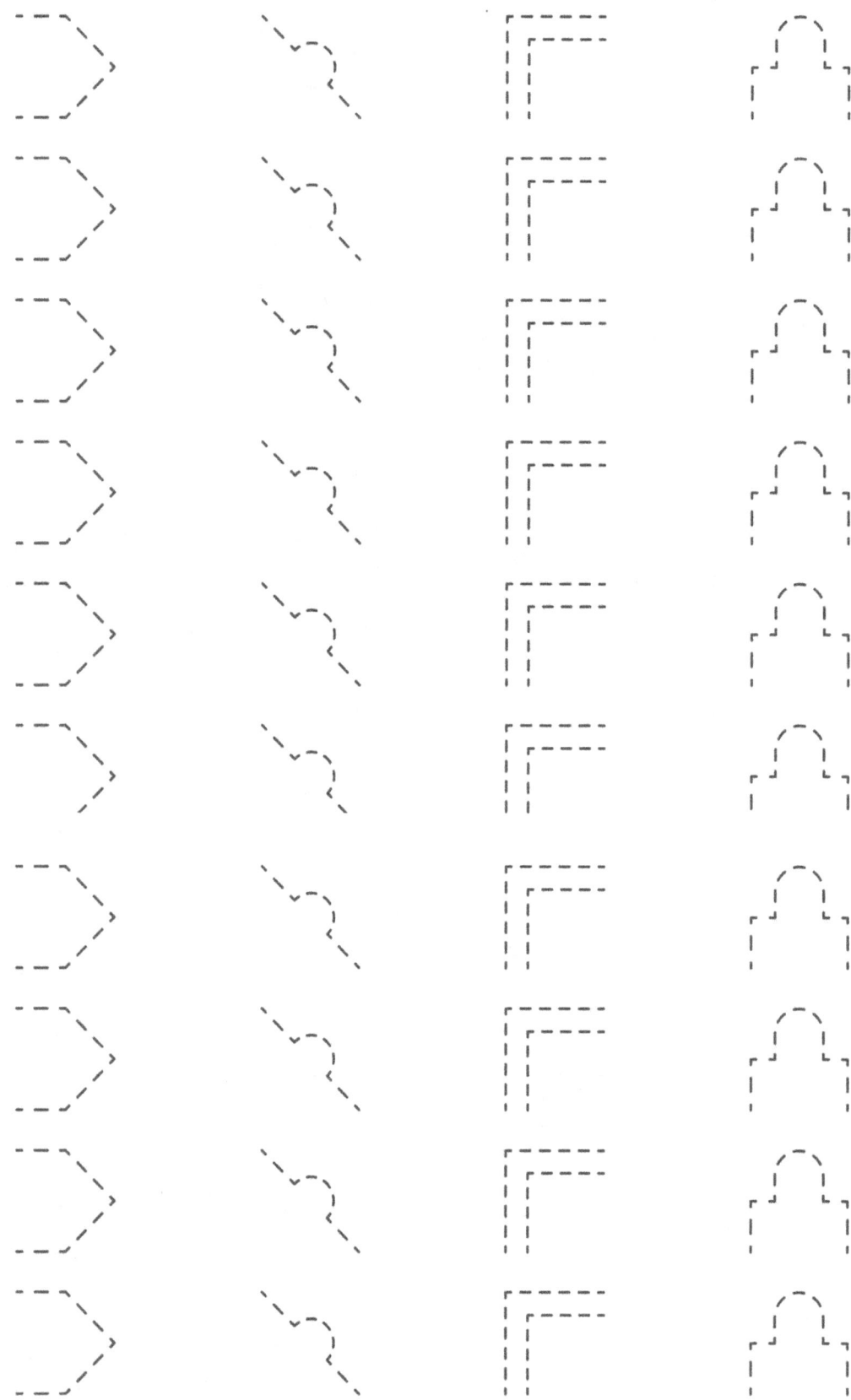

HANDWRITING PRE-PRACTICE

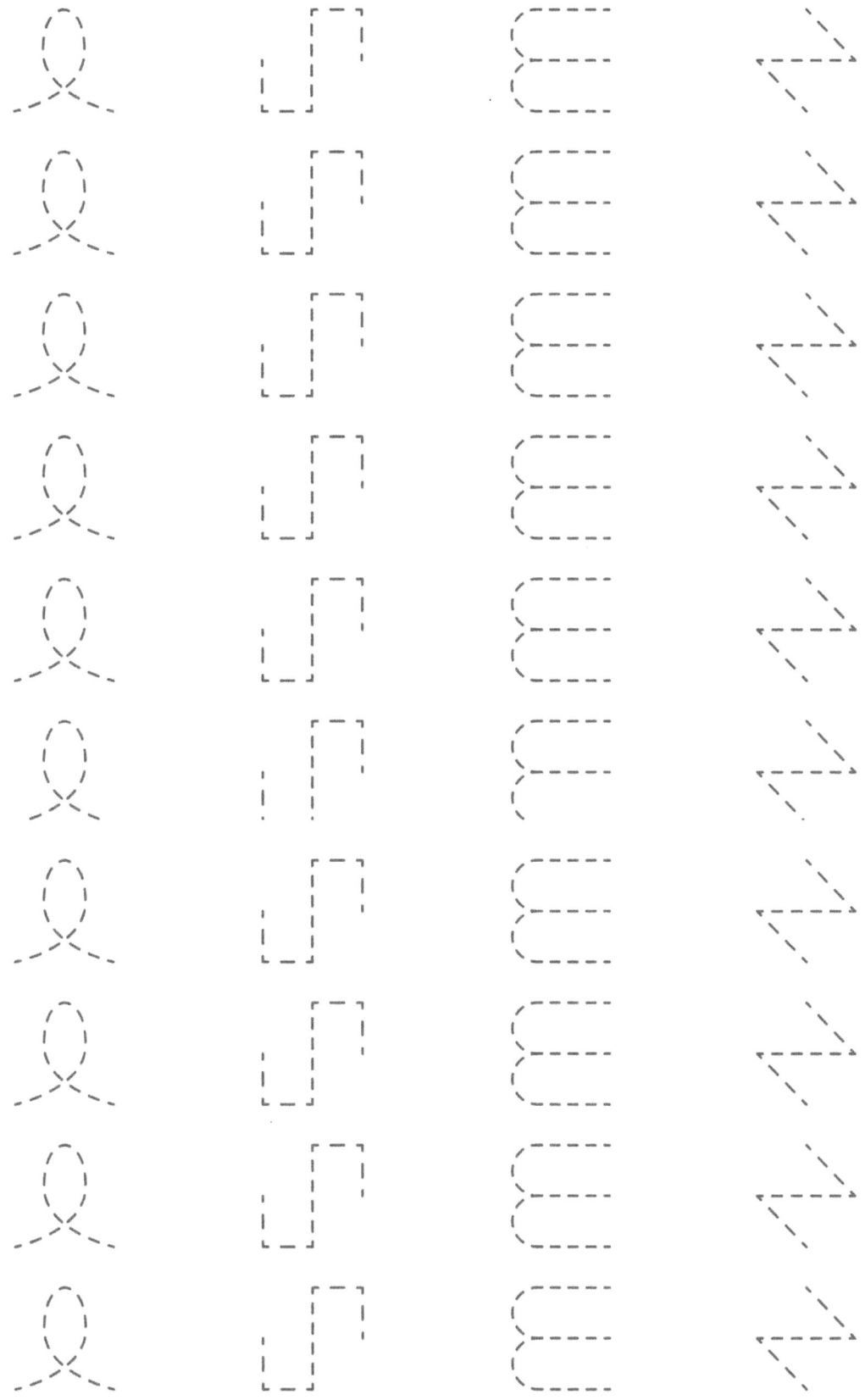

Aa

Anchor

Practice writing the uppercase letter A.

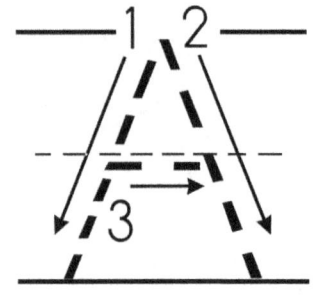
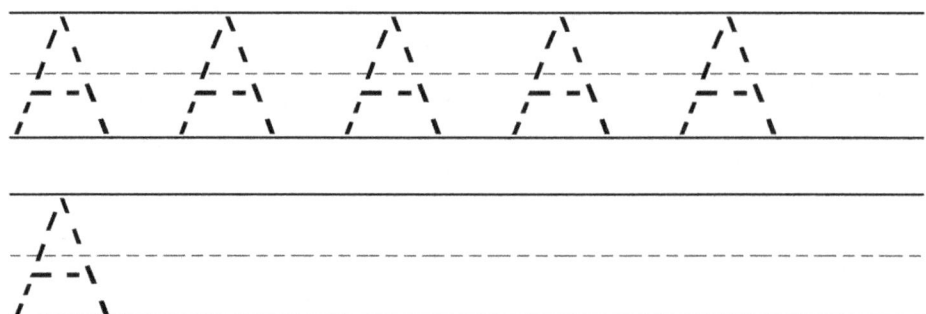

1

Color all the A letters.

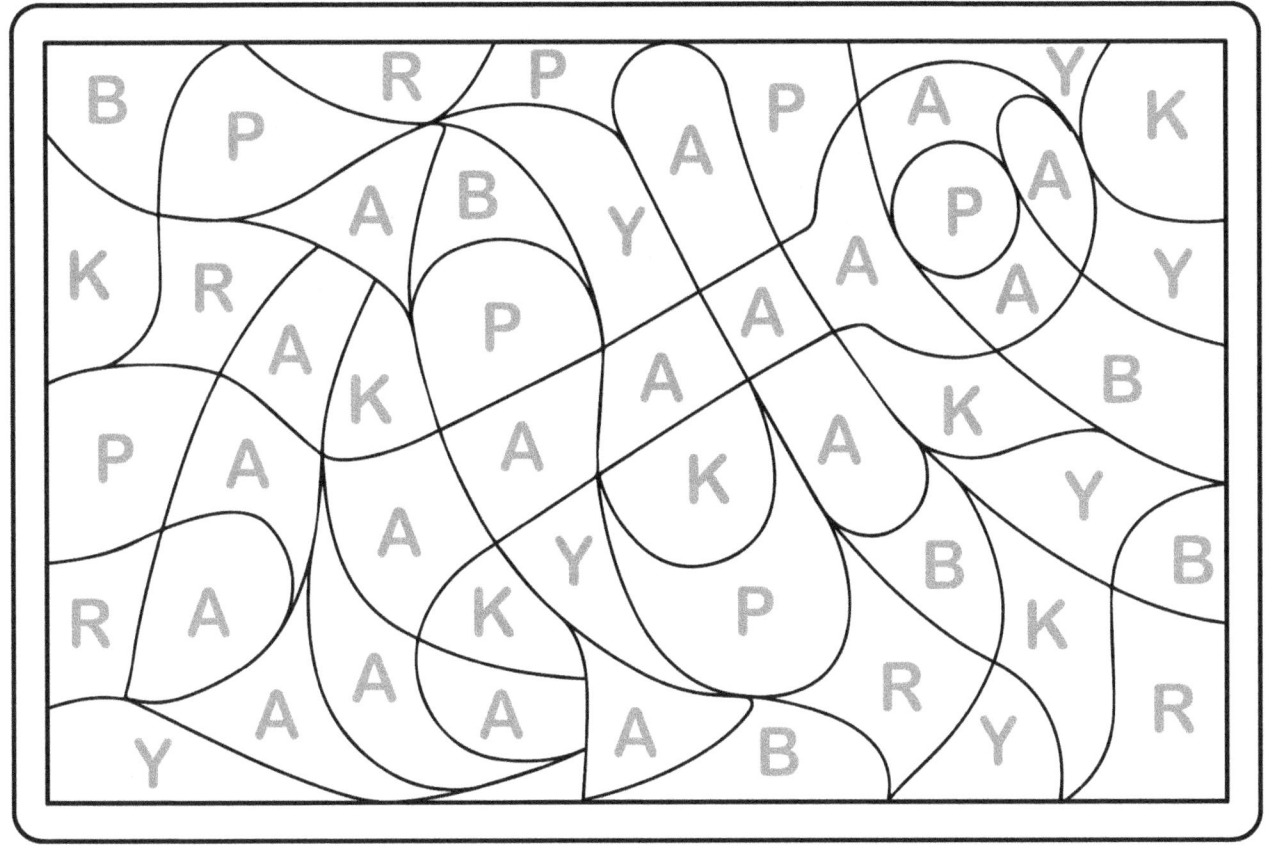

Practice writing the lowercase letter a.

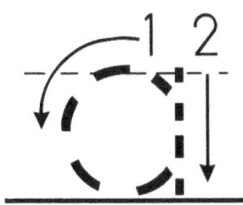
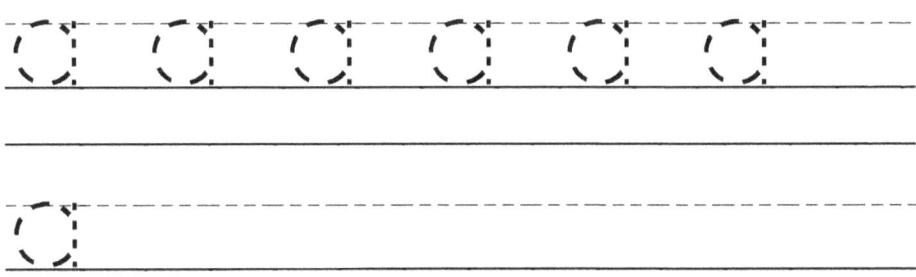

Bb

Butterfly

Practice writing the uppercase letter B.

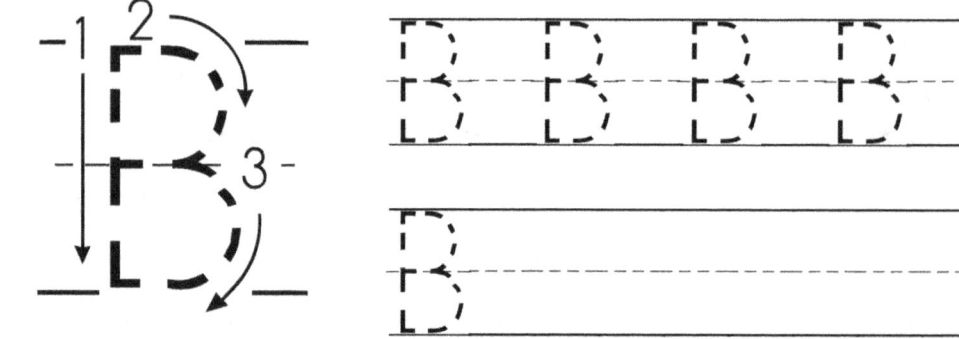

Bb

Color all the B letters.

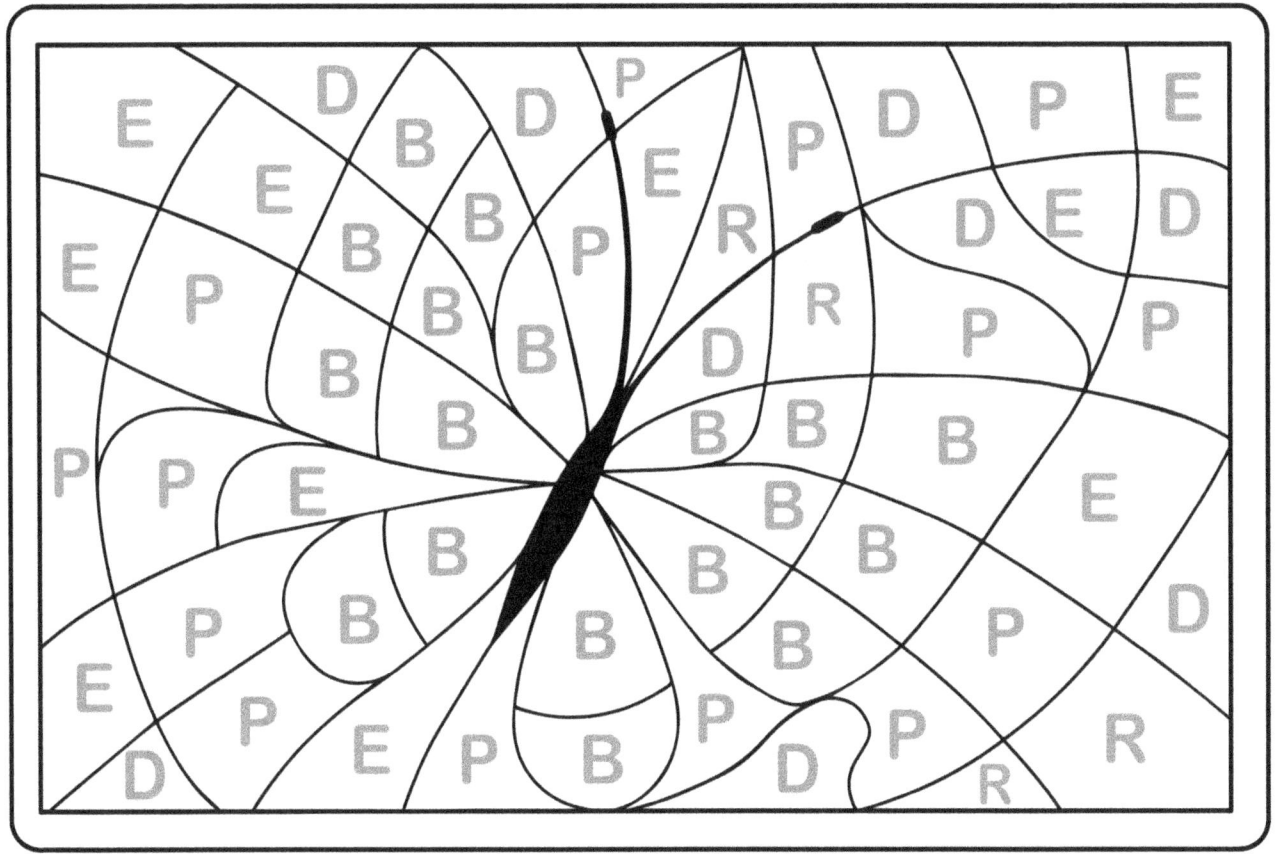

Practice writing the lowercase letter a.

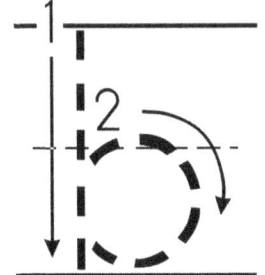
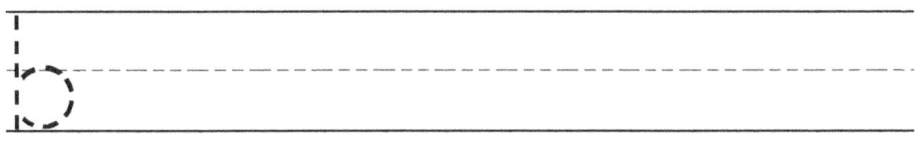

4

Cc

Cup

Practice writing the uppercase letter C.

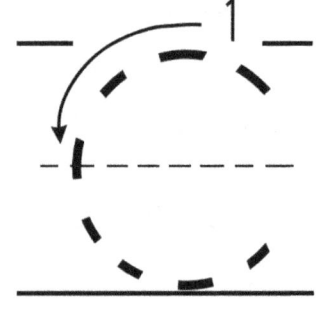 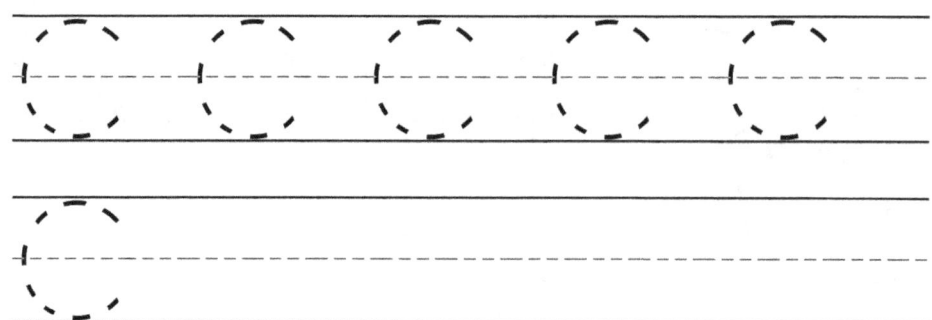

Color all the C letters.

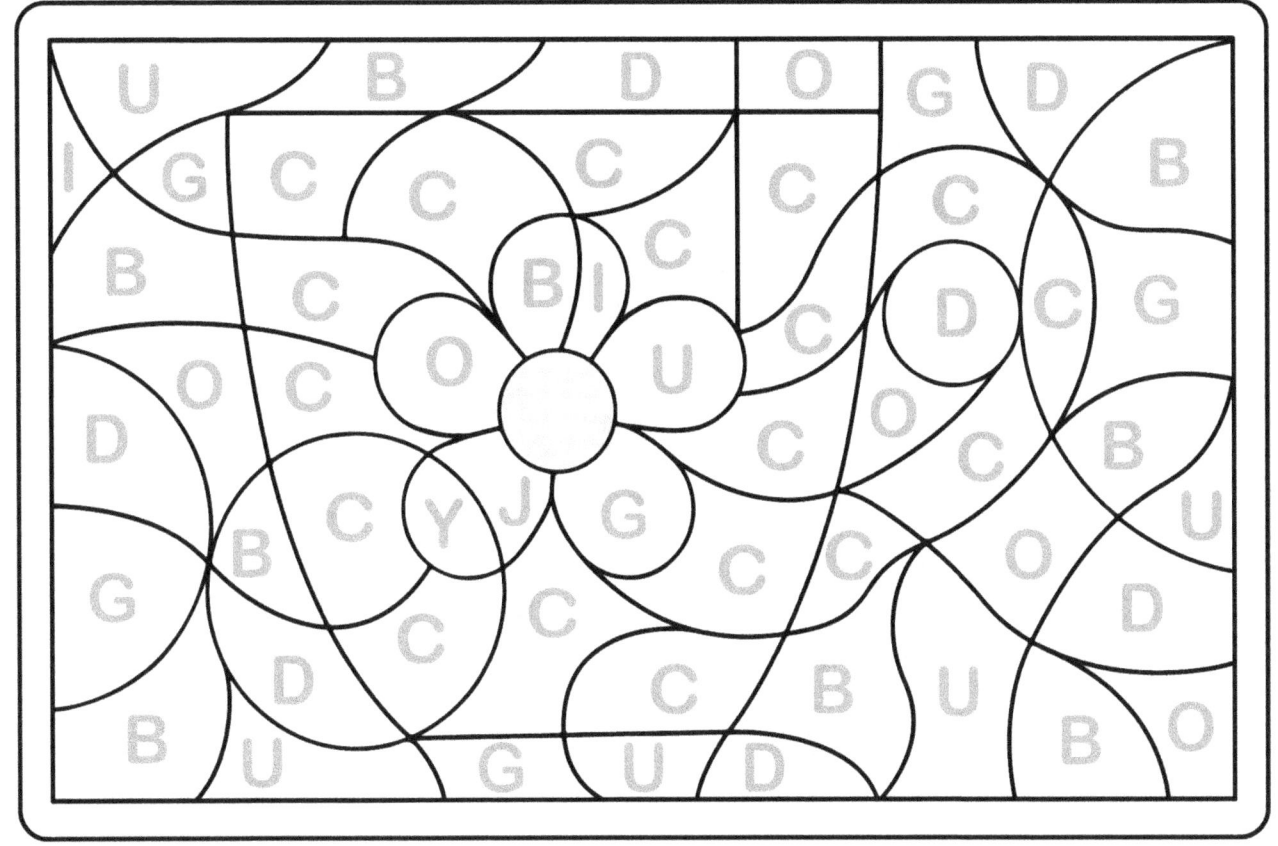

Practice writing the lowercase letter c.

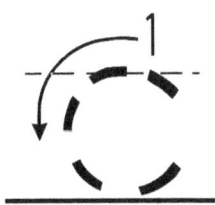
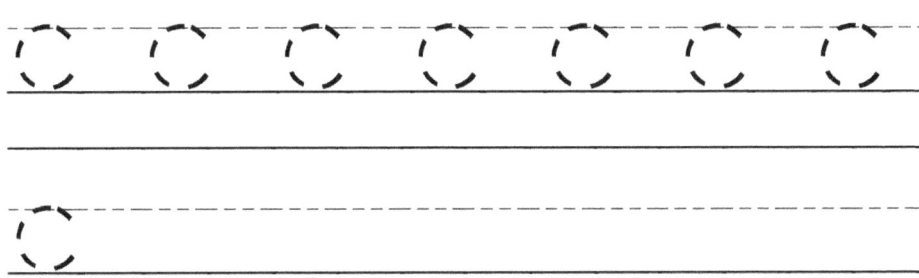

Dd

Dog

Practice writing the uppercase letter D.

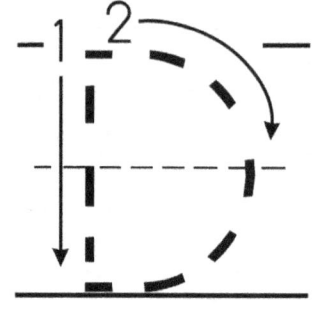

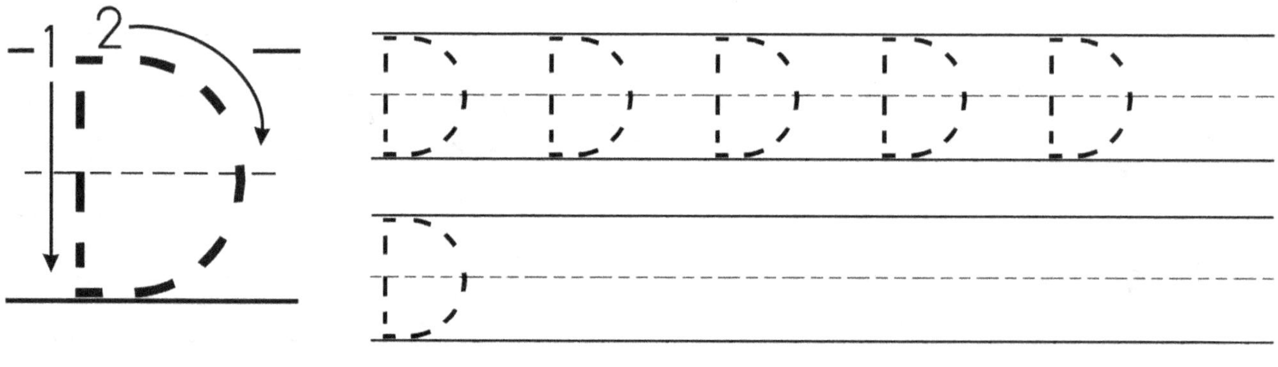

Dd

Color all the D letters.

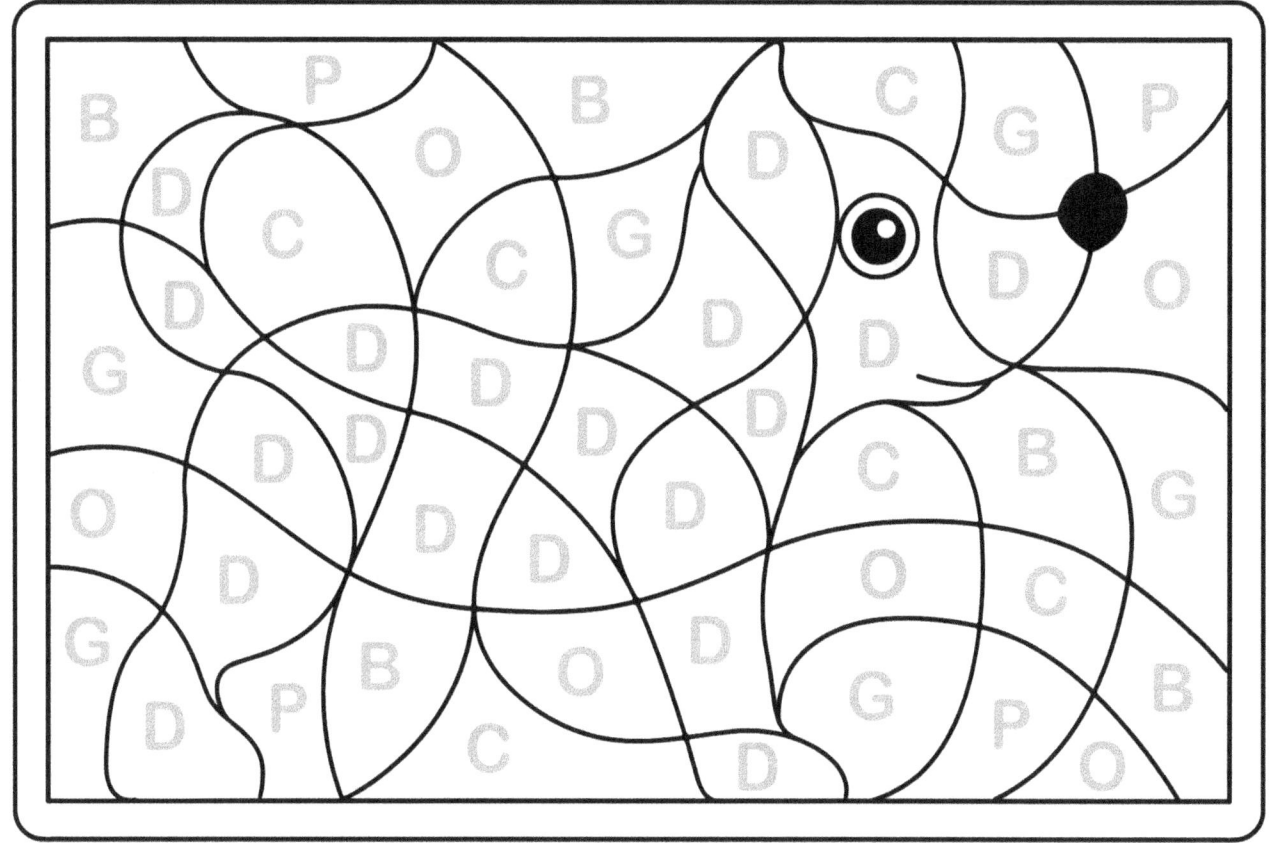

Practice writing the lowercase letter d.

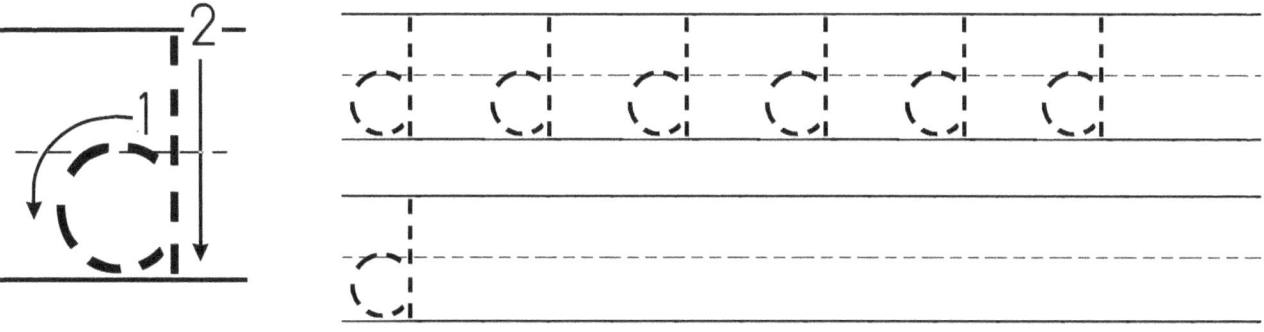

Ee

Elephant

Practice writing the uppercase letter E.

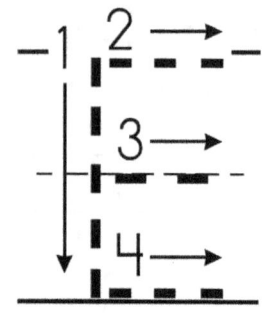
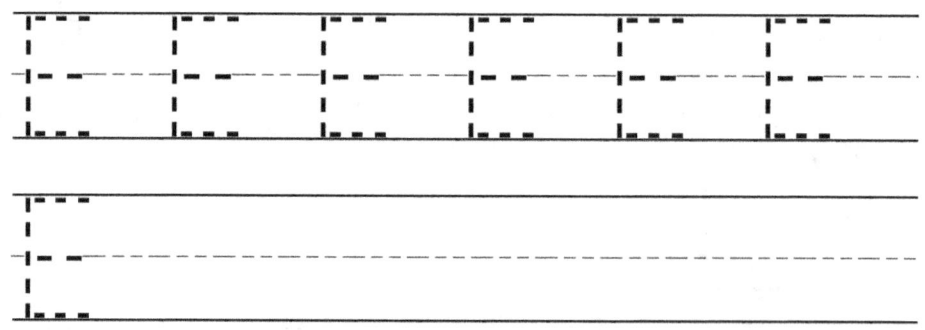

Color all the E letters.

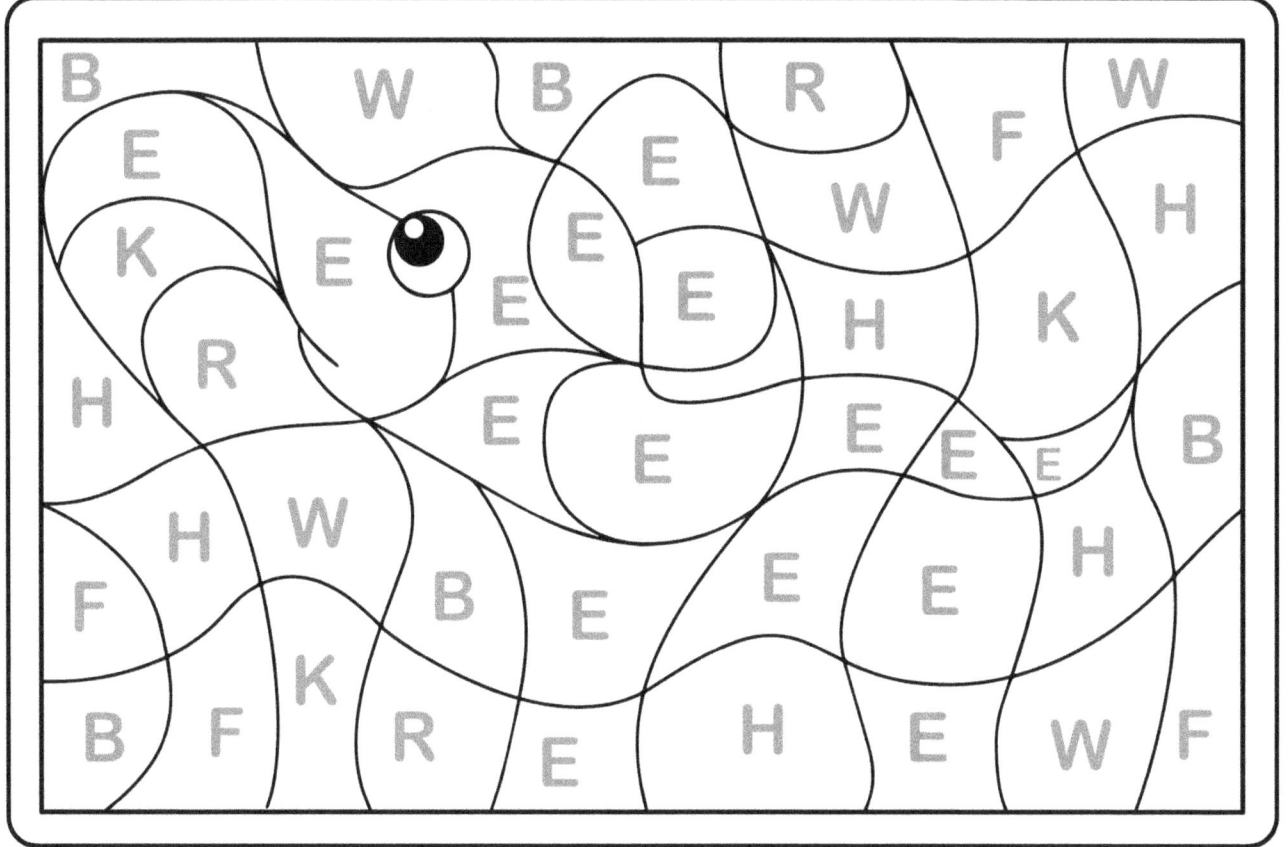

Practice writing the lowercase letter e.

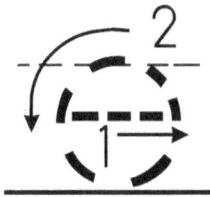

Ff

Flag

Practice writing the uppercase letter F.

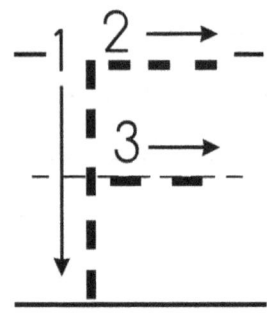
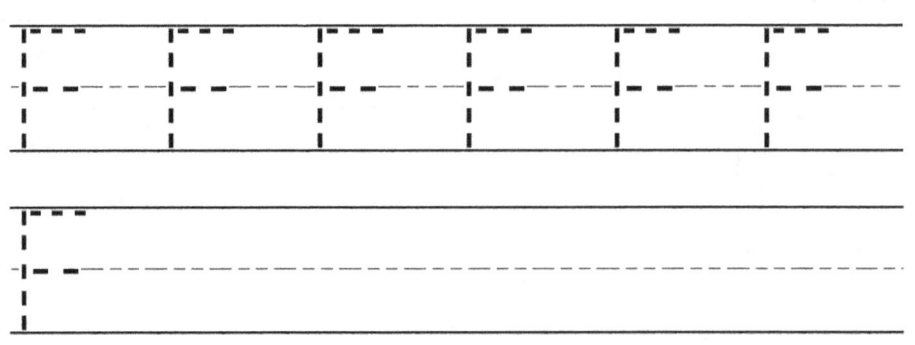

Ff

Color all the F letters.

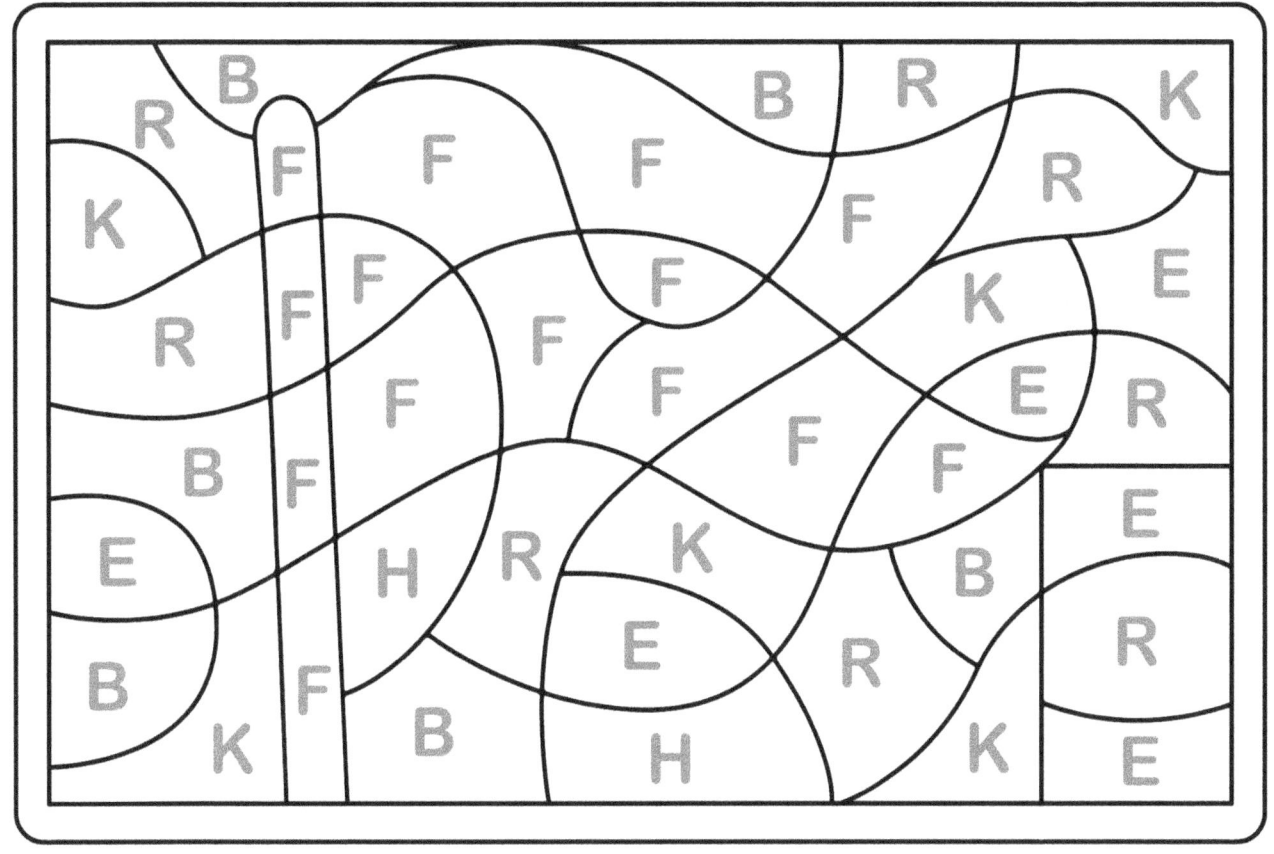

Practice writing the lowercase letter f.

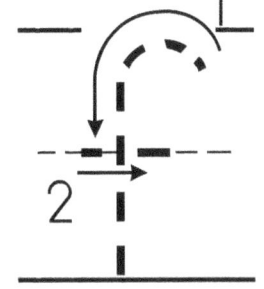
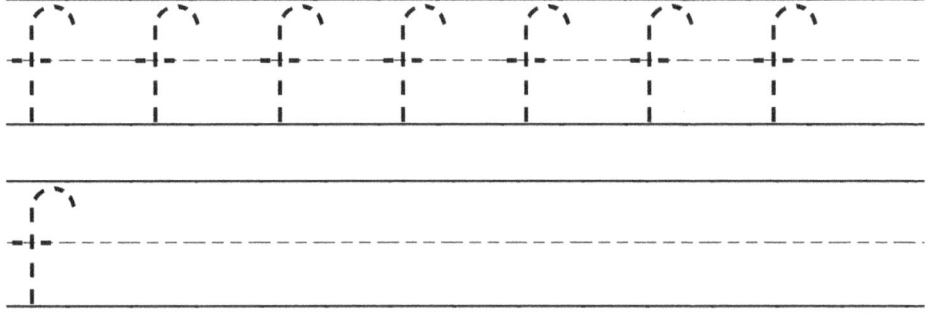

Gg

Gift

Practice writing the uppercase letter G.

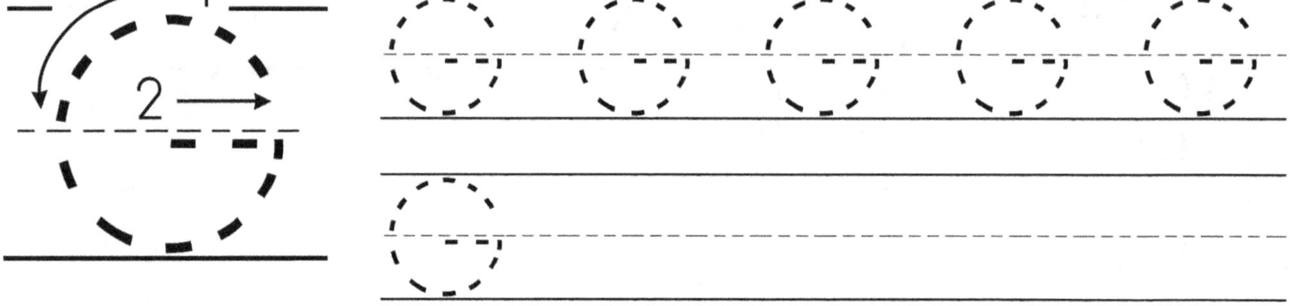

Color all the G letters.

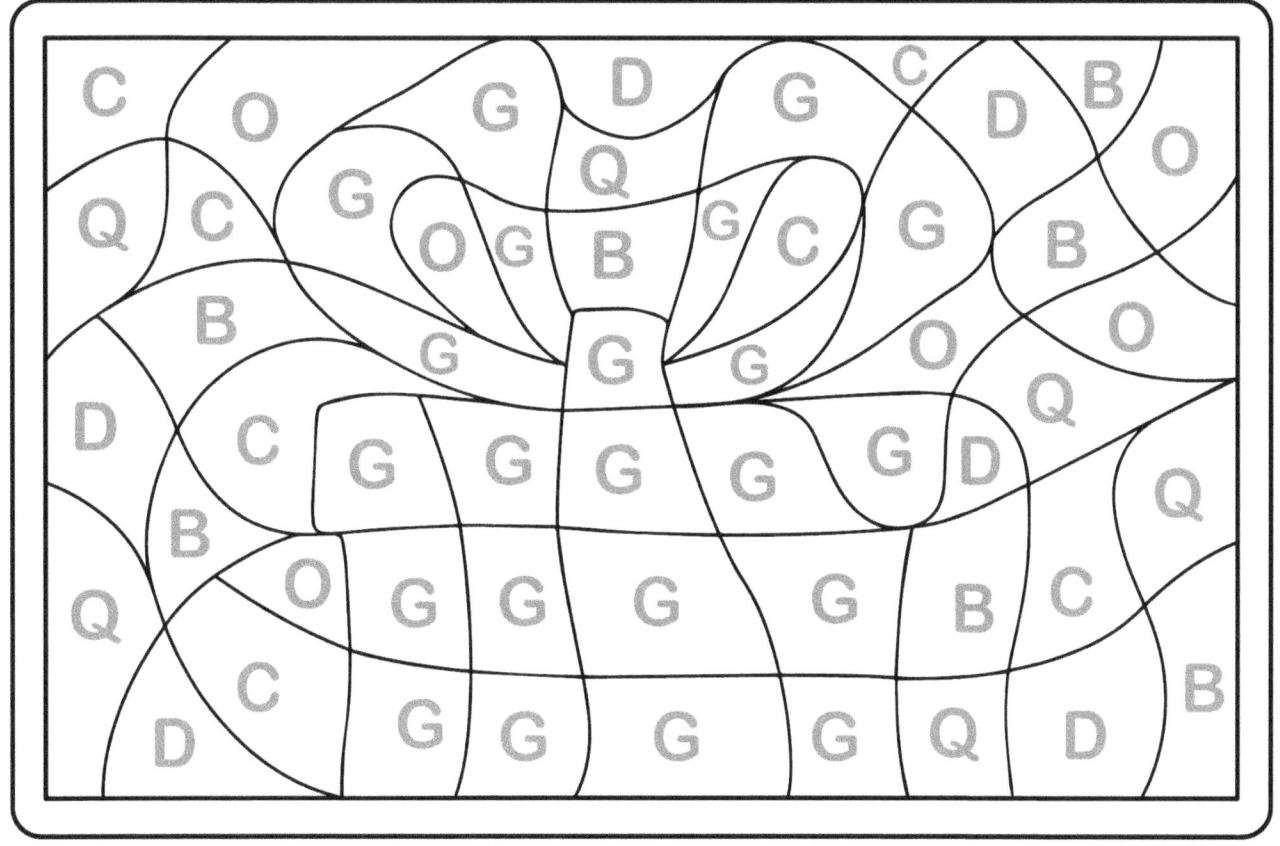

Practice writing the lowercase letter g.

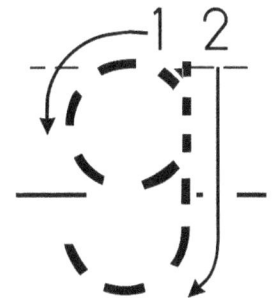
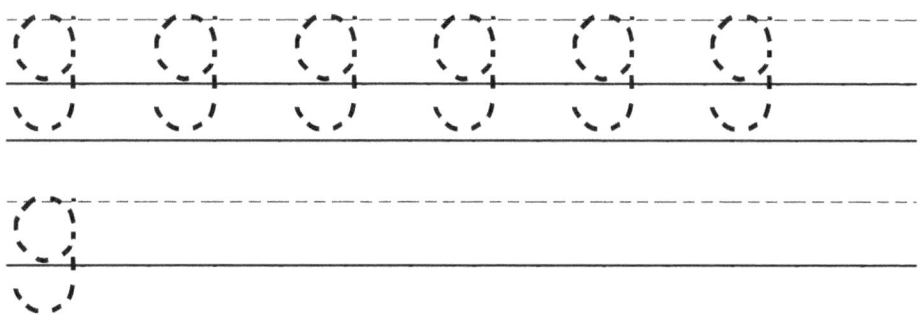

Hh

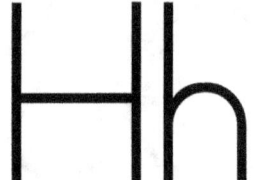

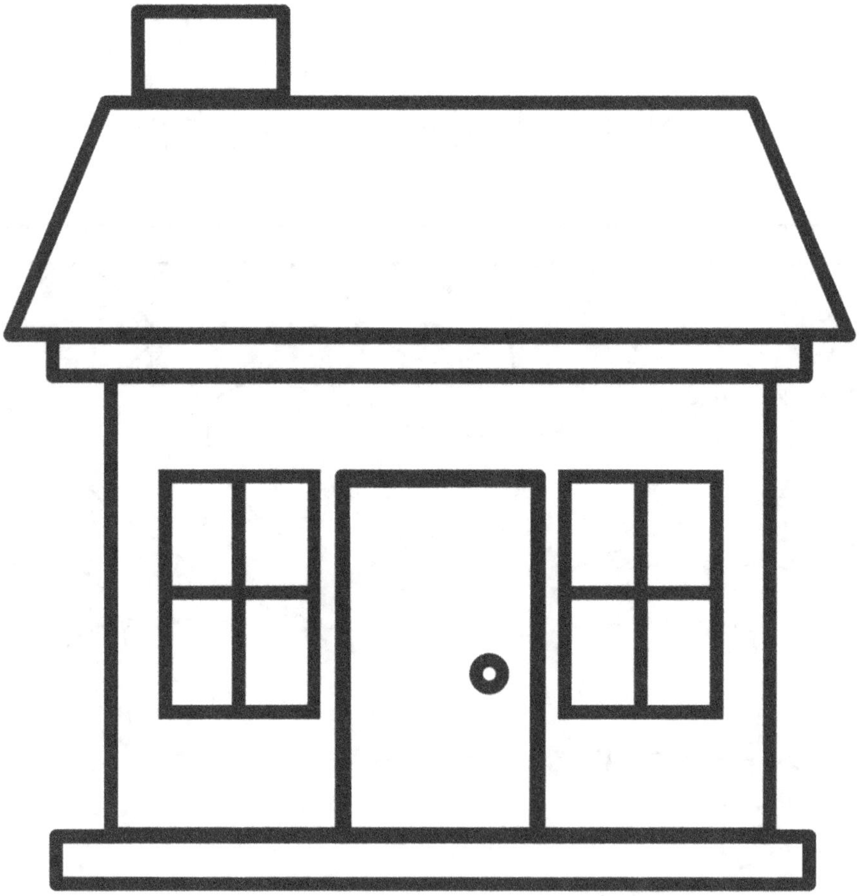

House

Practice writing the uppercase letter H.

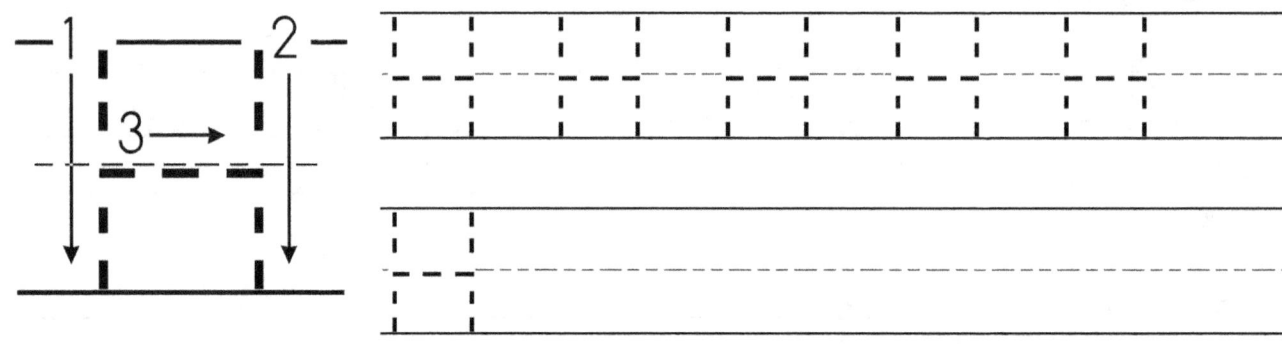

Color all the H letters.

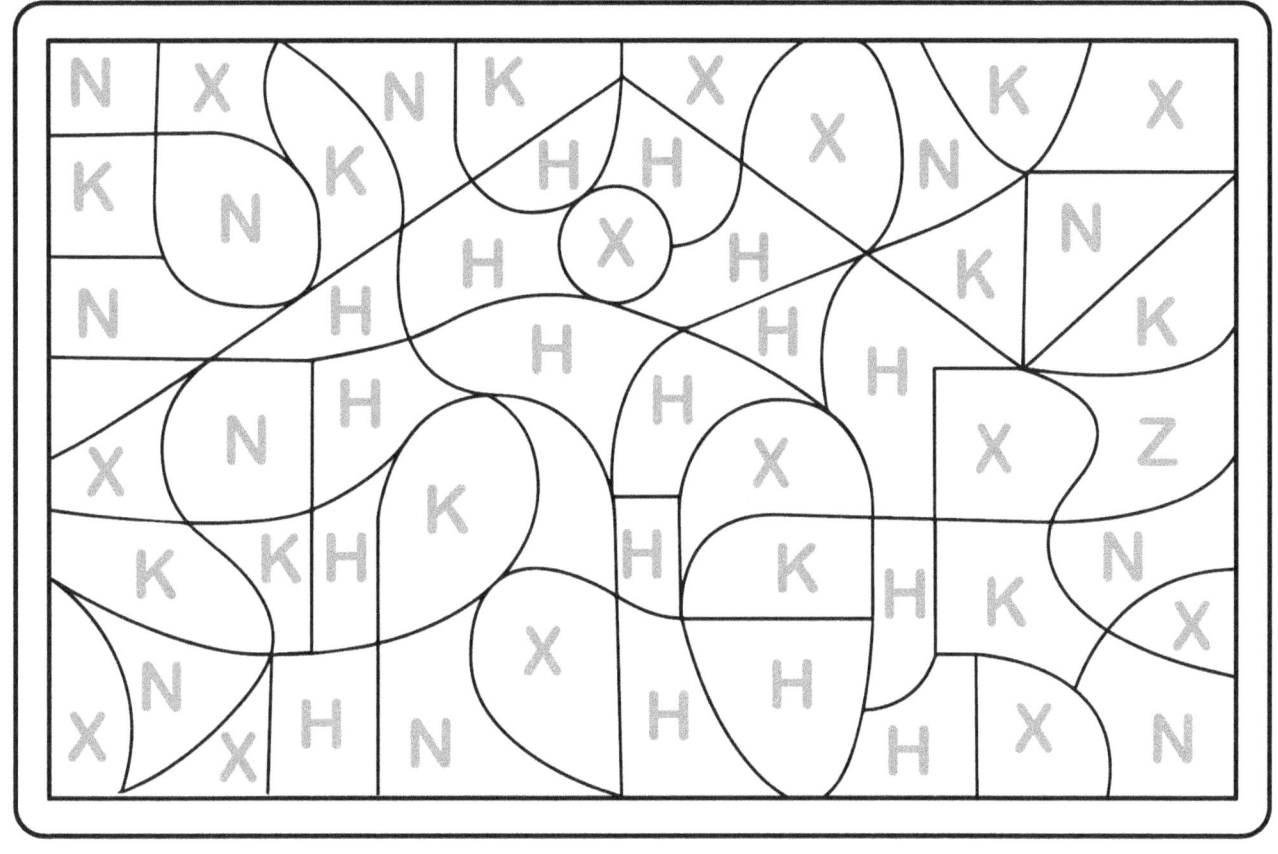

Practice writing the lowercase letter h.

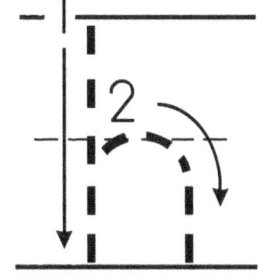
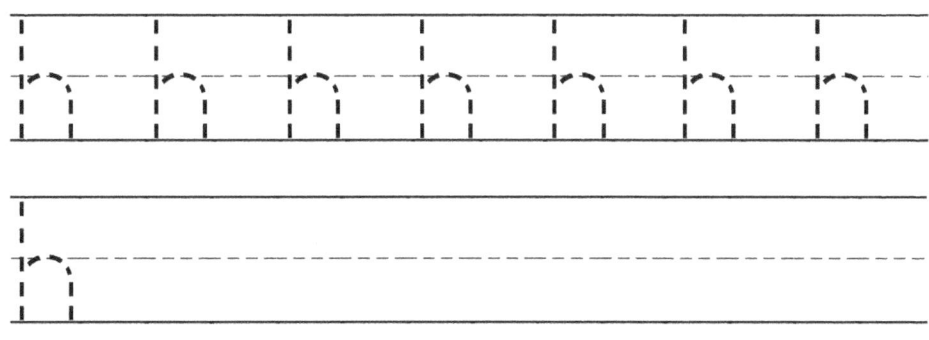

16

I i

Ice cream

Practice writing the uppercase letter I.

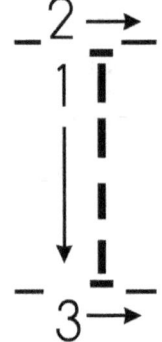
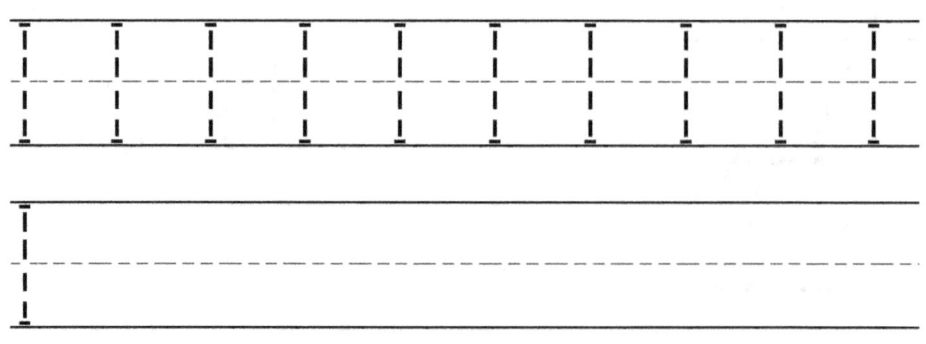

Ii

Color all the I letters.

Practice writing the lowercase letter i.

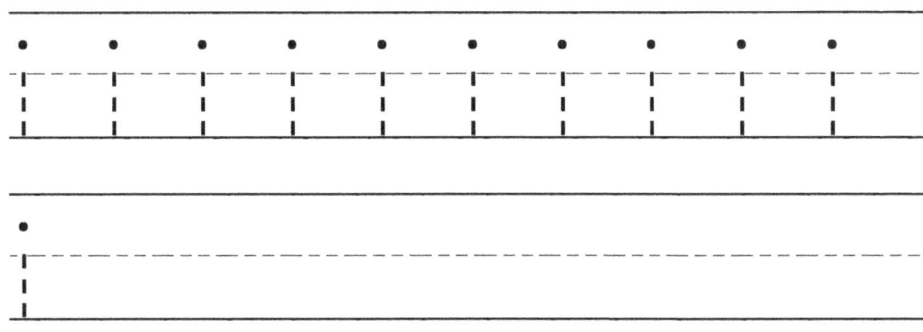

18

Jellyfish

Practice writing the uppercase letter J.

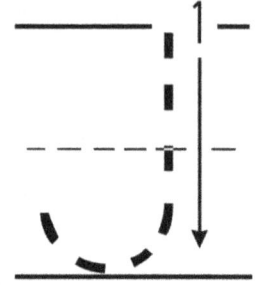

Jj

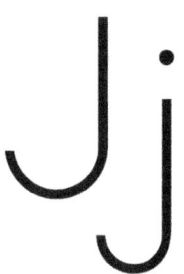

Color all the J letters.

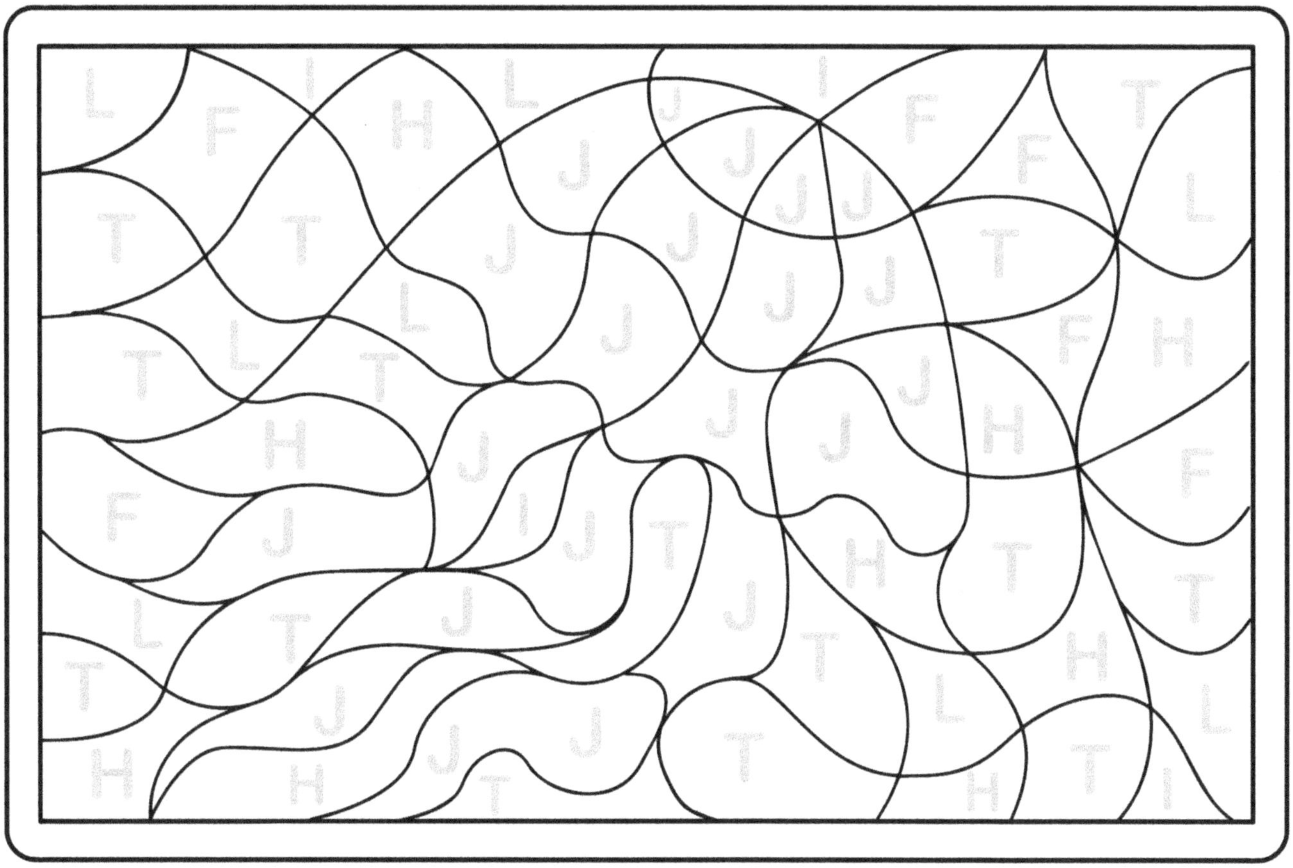

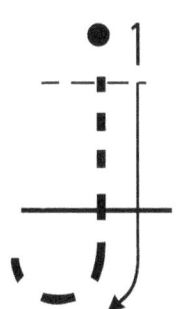

Practice writing the lowercase letter j.

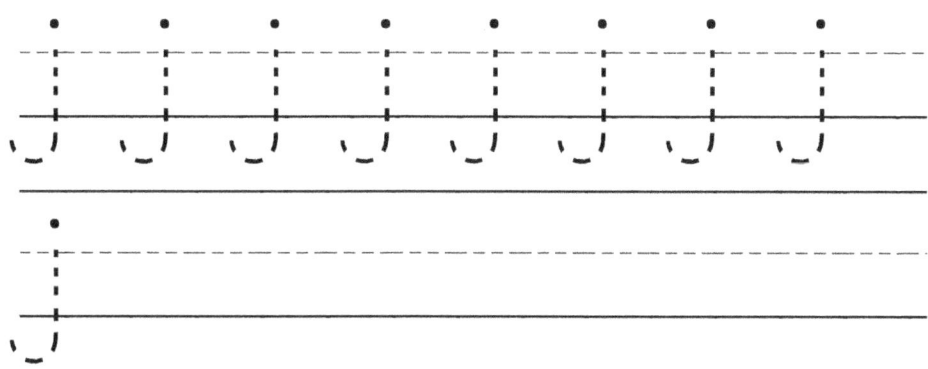

Kk

Key

Practice writing the uppercase letter K.

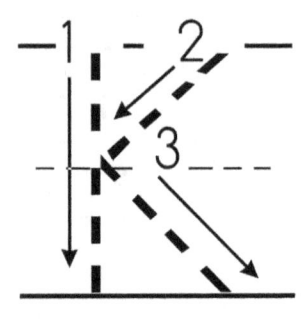
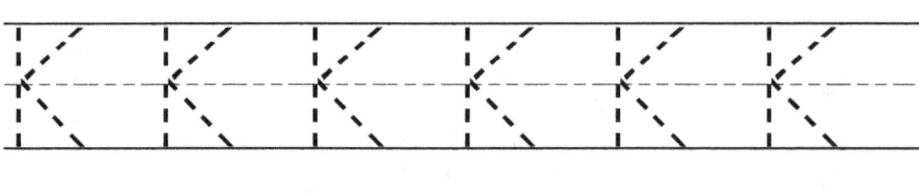
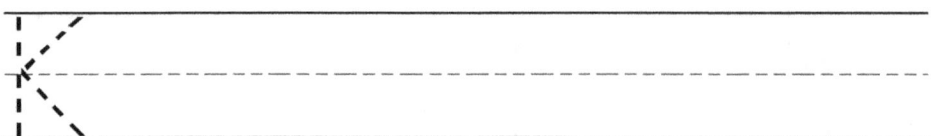

Color all the K letters.

Practice writing the lowercase letter k.

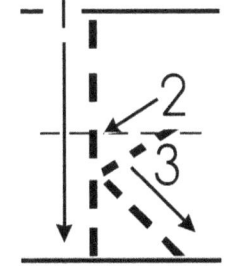
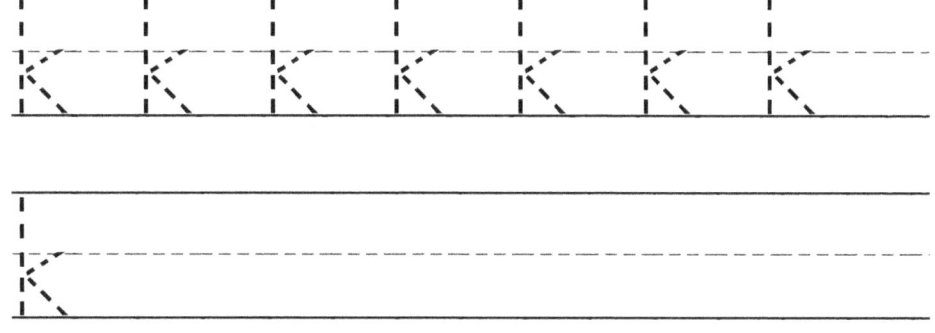

22

Ll

Leaf

Practice writing the uppercase letter L.

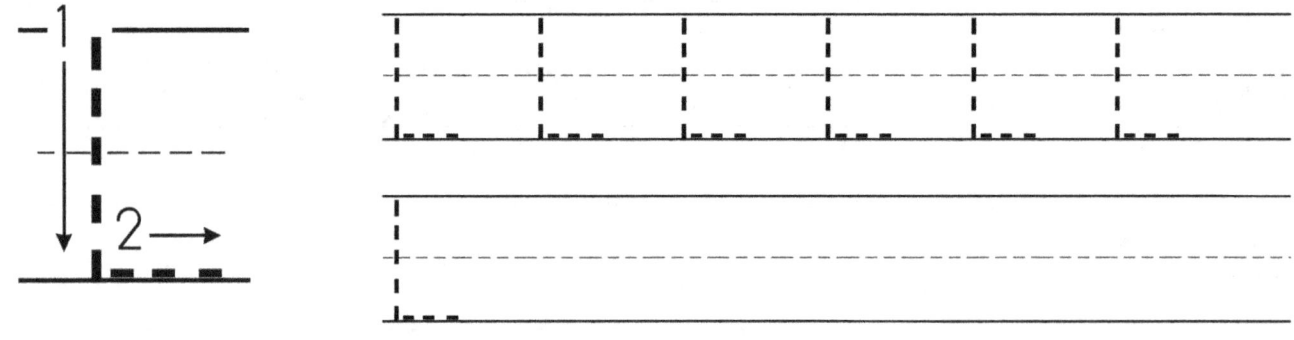

Color all the L letters.

Practice writing the lowercase letter l.

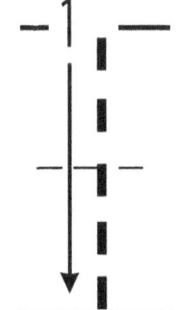

24

Mm

Mittens

Practice writing the uppercase letter M.

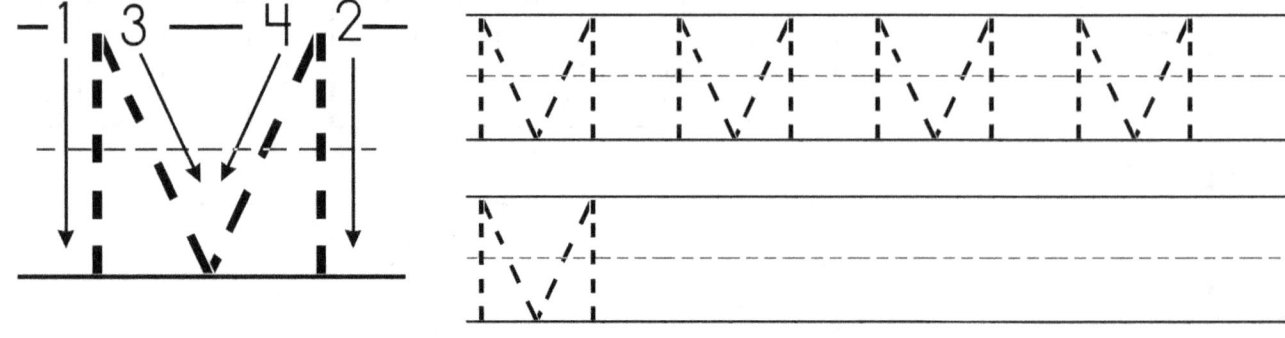

Color all the M letters.

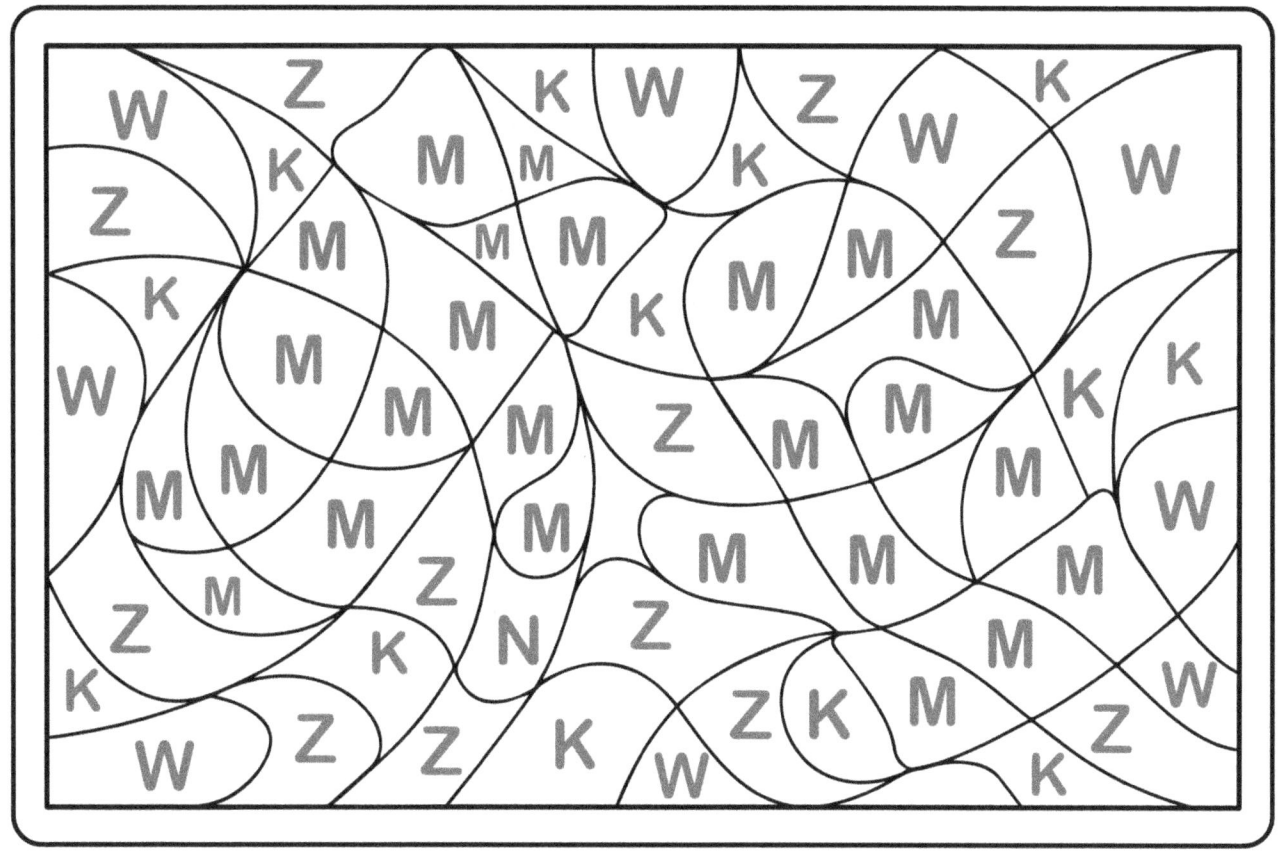

Practice writing the lowercase letter m.

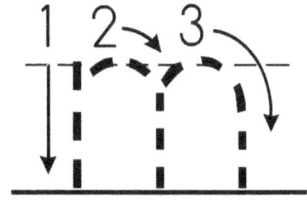

Nn

Notes

Practice writing the uppercase letter N.

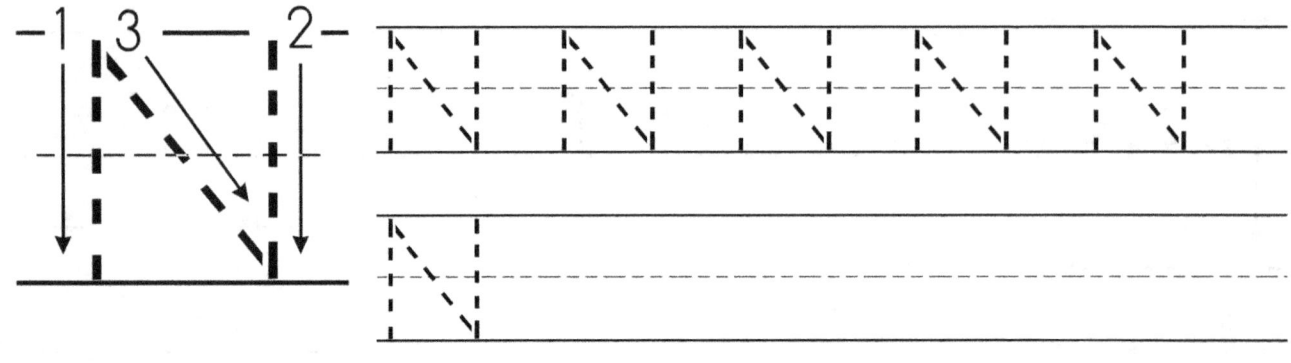

27

Color all the N letters.

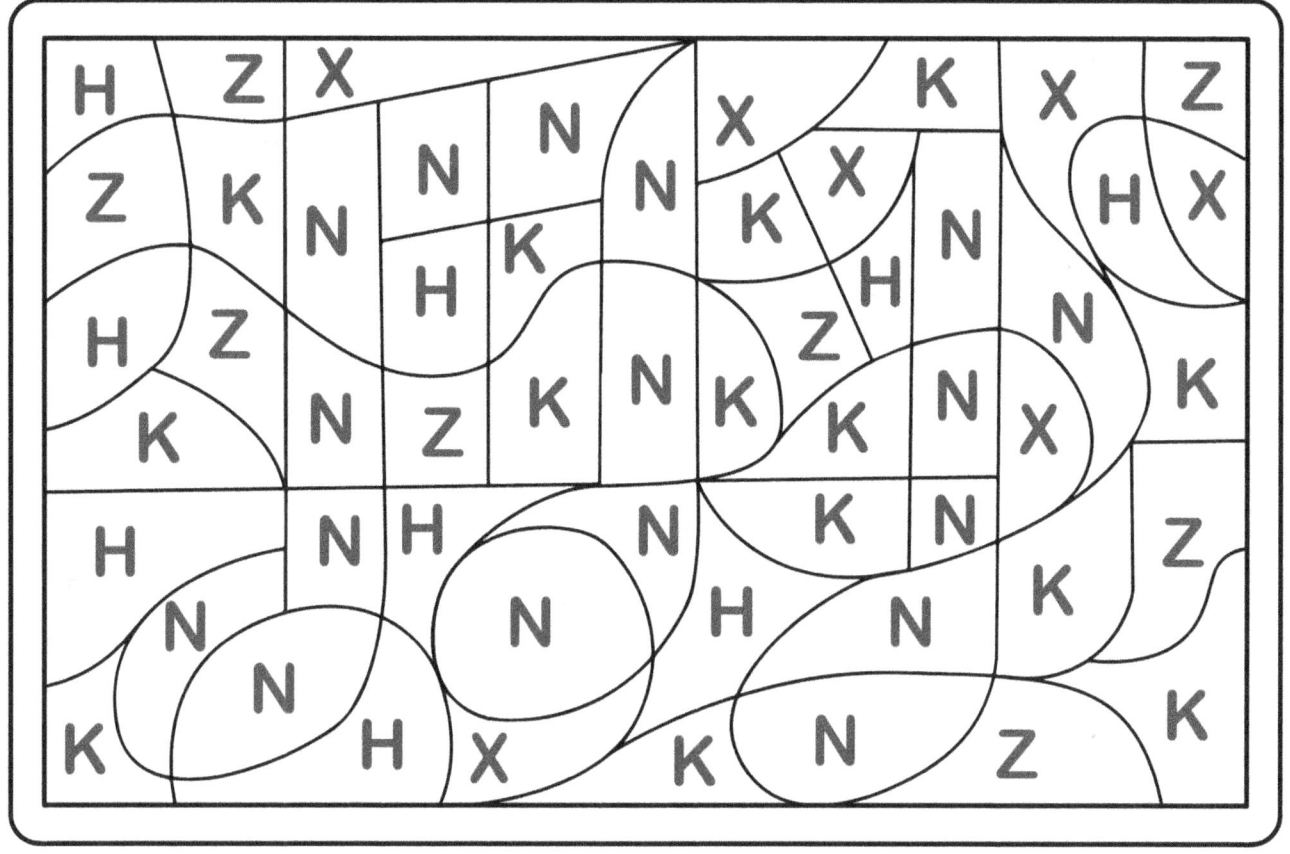

Practice writing the lowercase letter n.

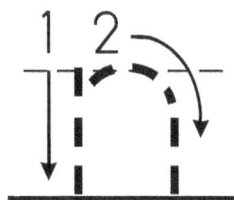
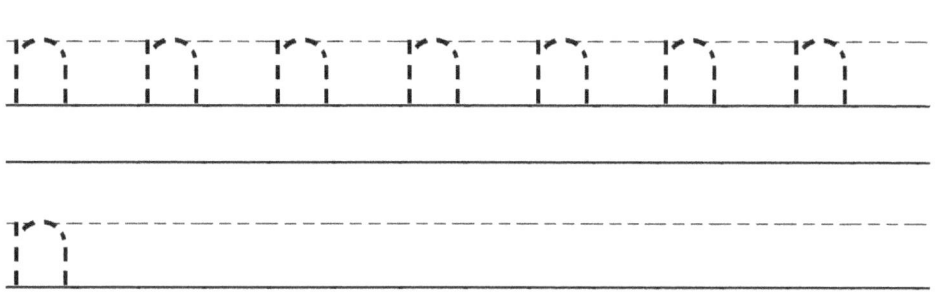

Oo

Octopus

Practice writing the uppercase letter O.

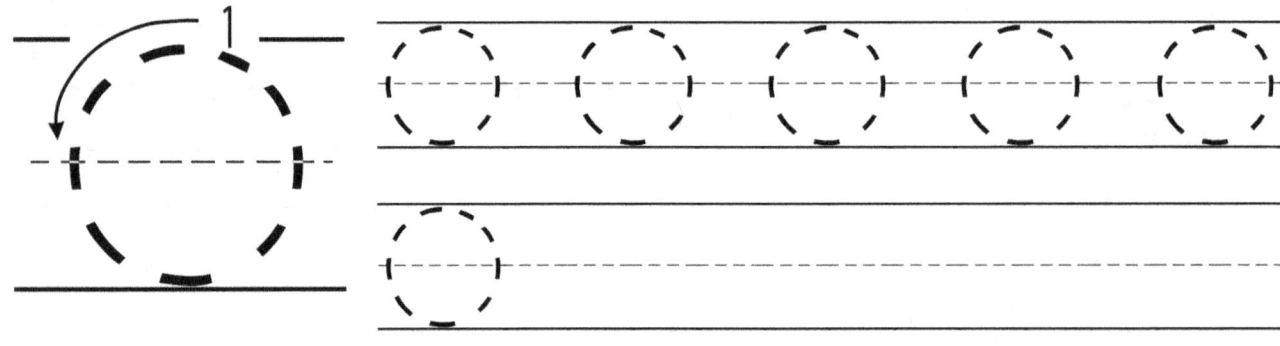

29

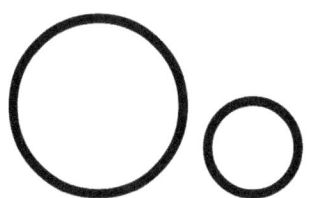

Color all the O letters.

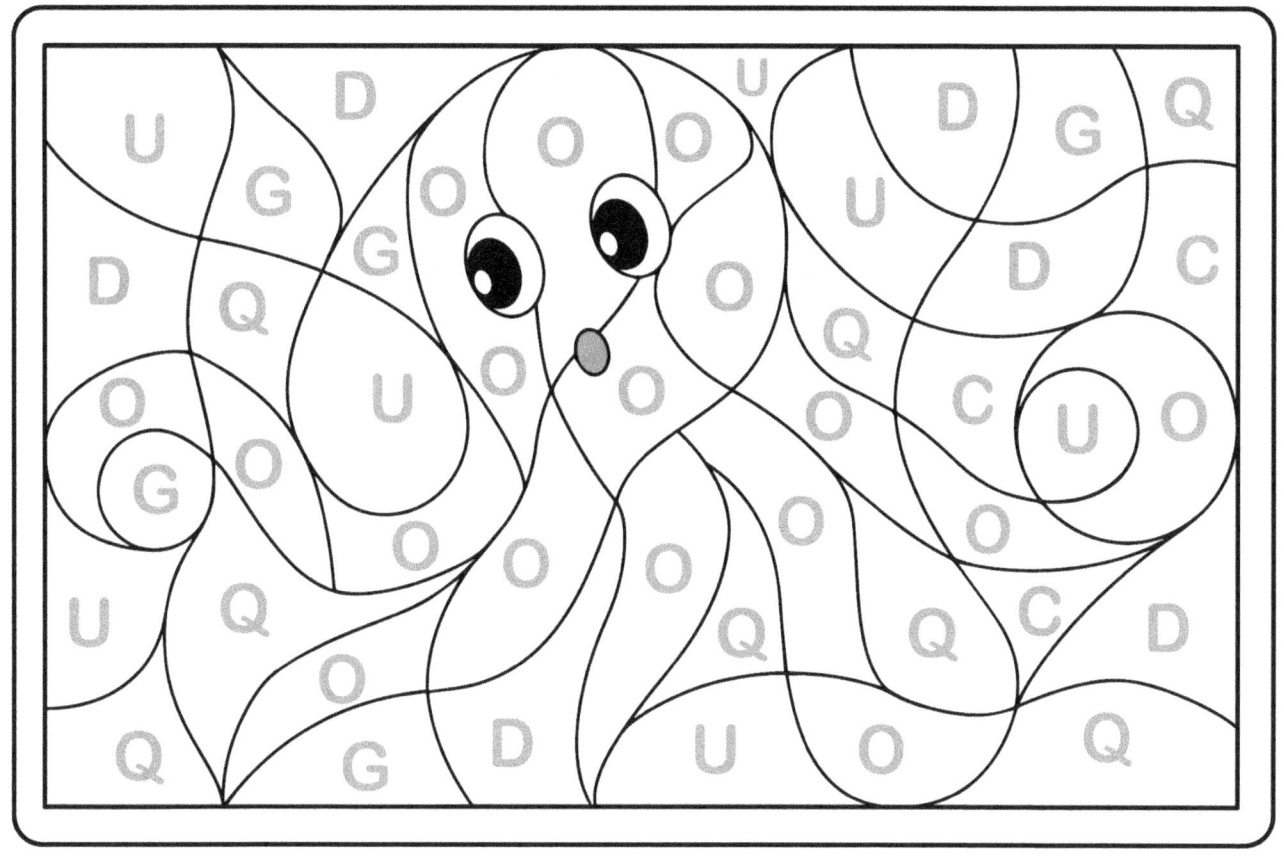

Practice writing the lowercase letter o.

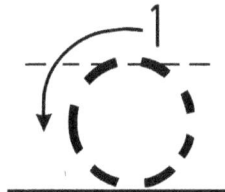

30

Pp

Plane

Practice writing the uppercase letter P.

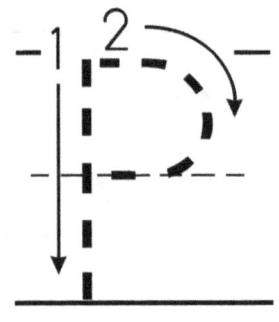

Color all the P letters.

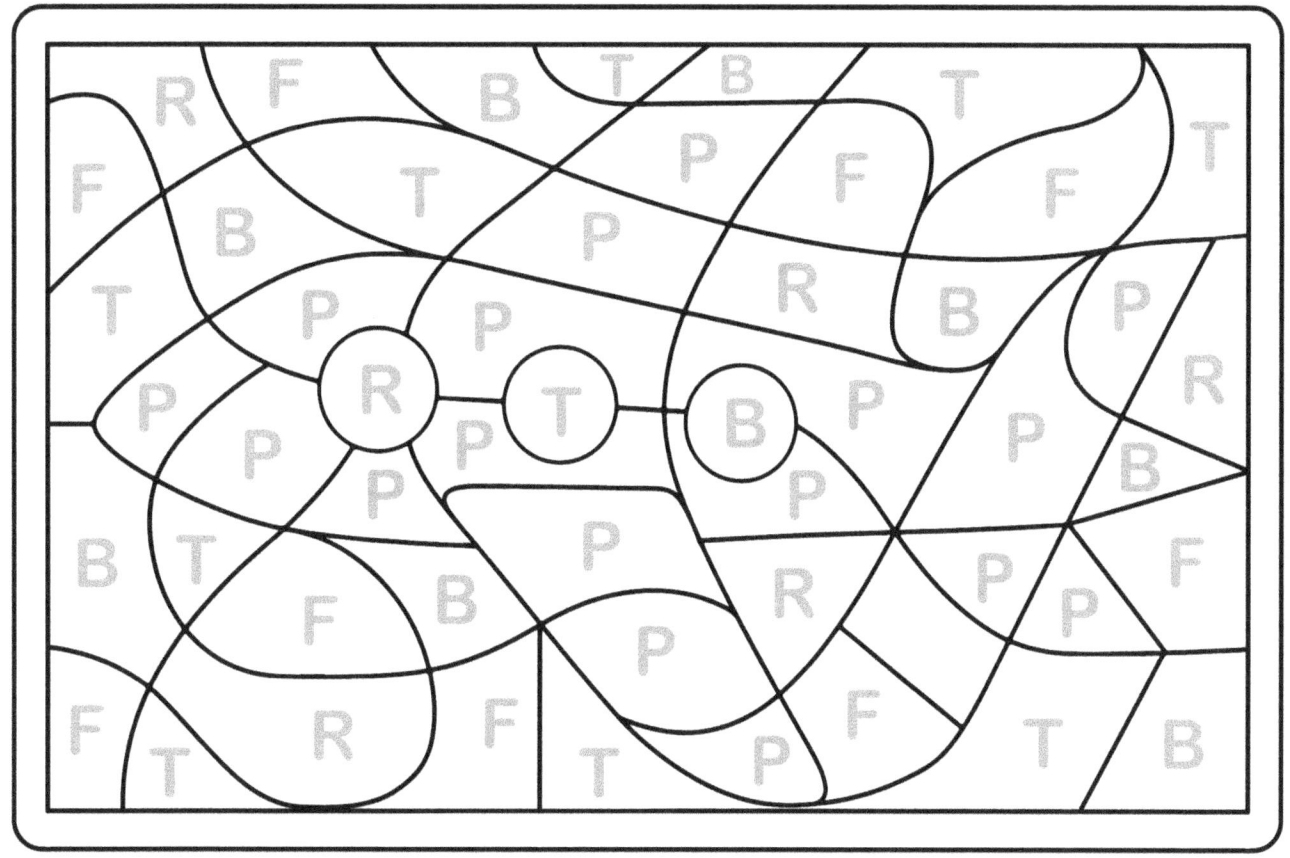

Practice writing the lowercase letter p.

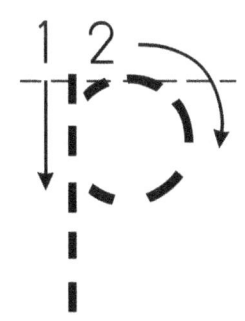

Qq

Quail

Practice writing the uppercase letter Q.

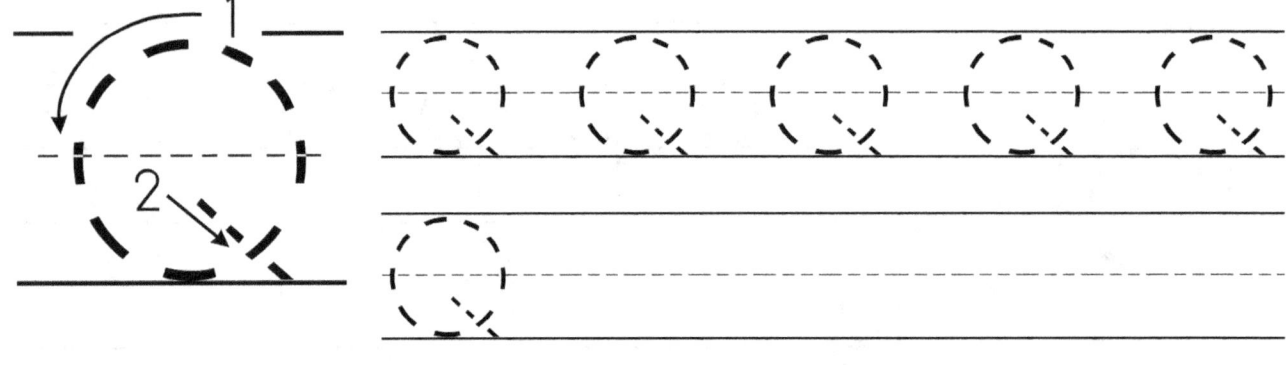

33

Color all the Q letters.

Practice writing the lowercase letter q.

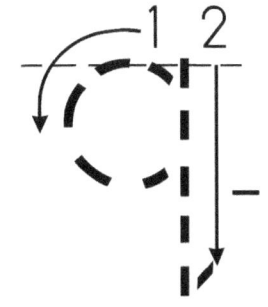

34

Rr

Rabbit

Practice writing the uppercase letter R.

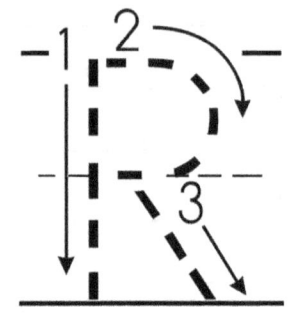

Color all the R letters.

Practice writing the lowercase letter r.

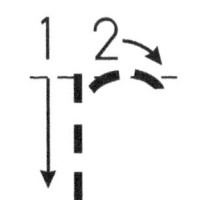
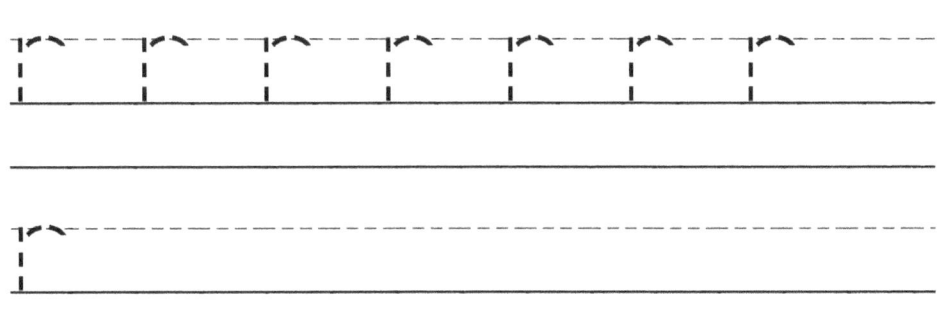

Ss

Snake

Practice writing the uppercase letter S.

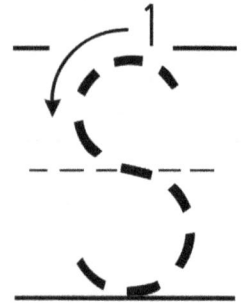

S S S S S S S

S

37

Ss

Color all the S letters.

Practice writing the lowercase letter s.

Tt

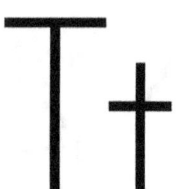

Teapot

Practice writing the uppercase letter T.

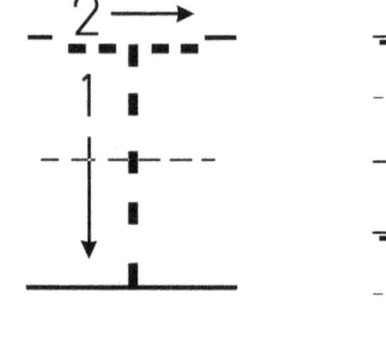

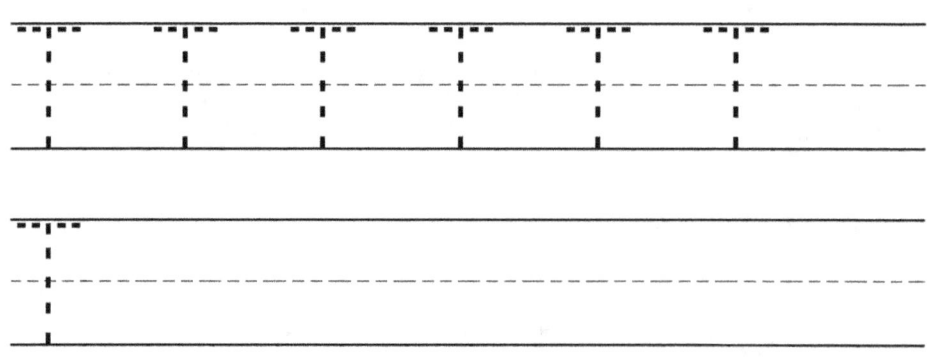

39

T t

Color all the T letters.

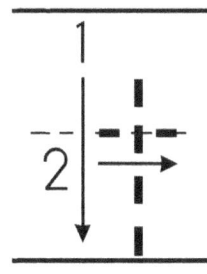

Practice writing the lower case letter t.

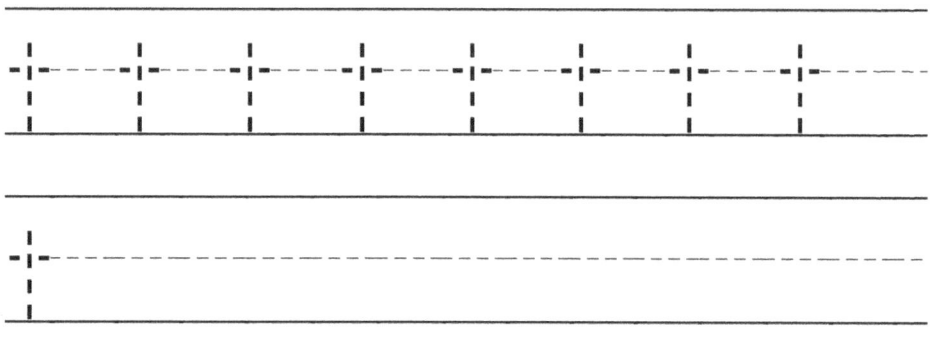

Uu

Umbrella

Practice writing the uppercase letter U.

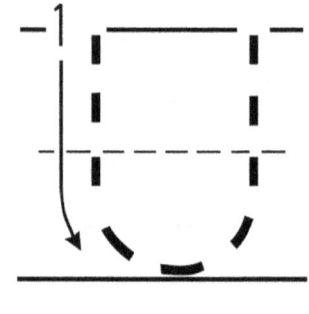
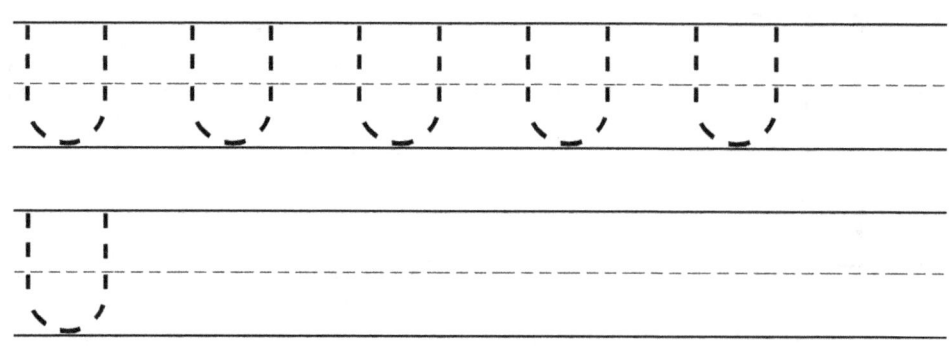

41

Color all the U letters.

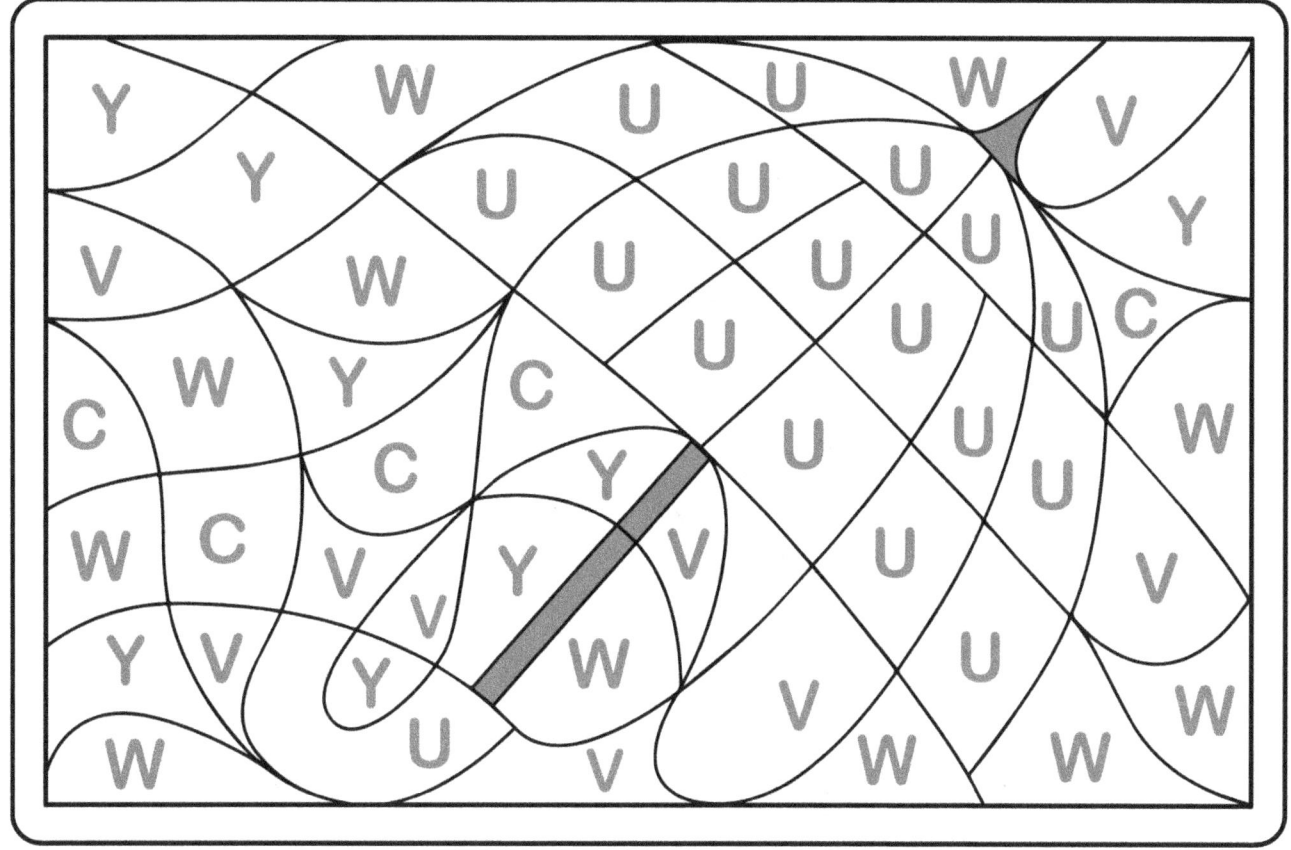

Practice writing the lowercase letter u.

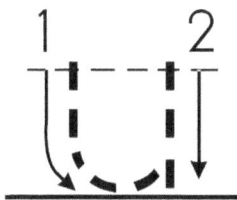
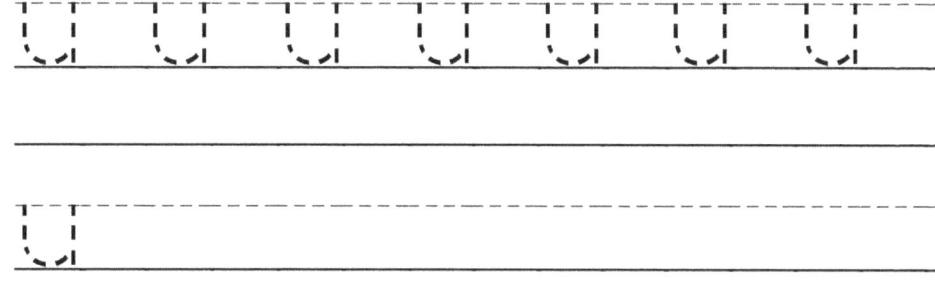

Vv

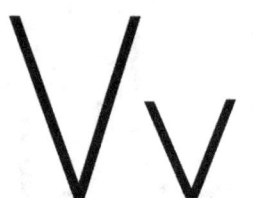

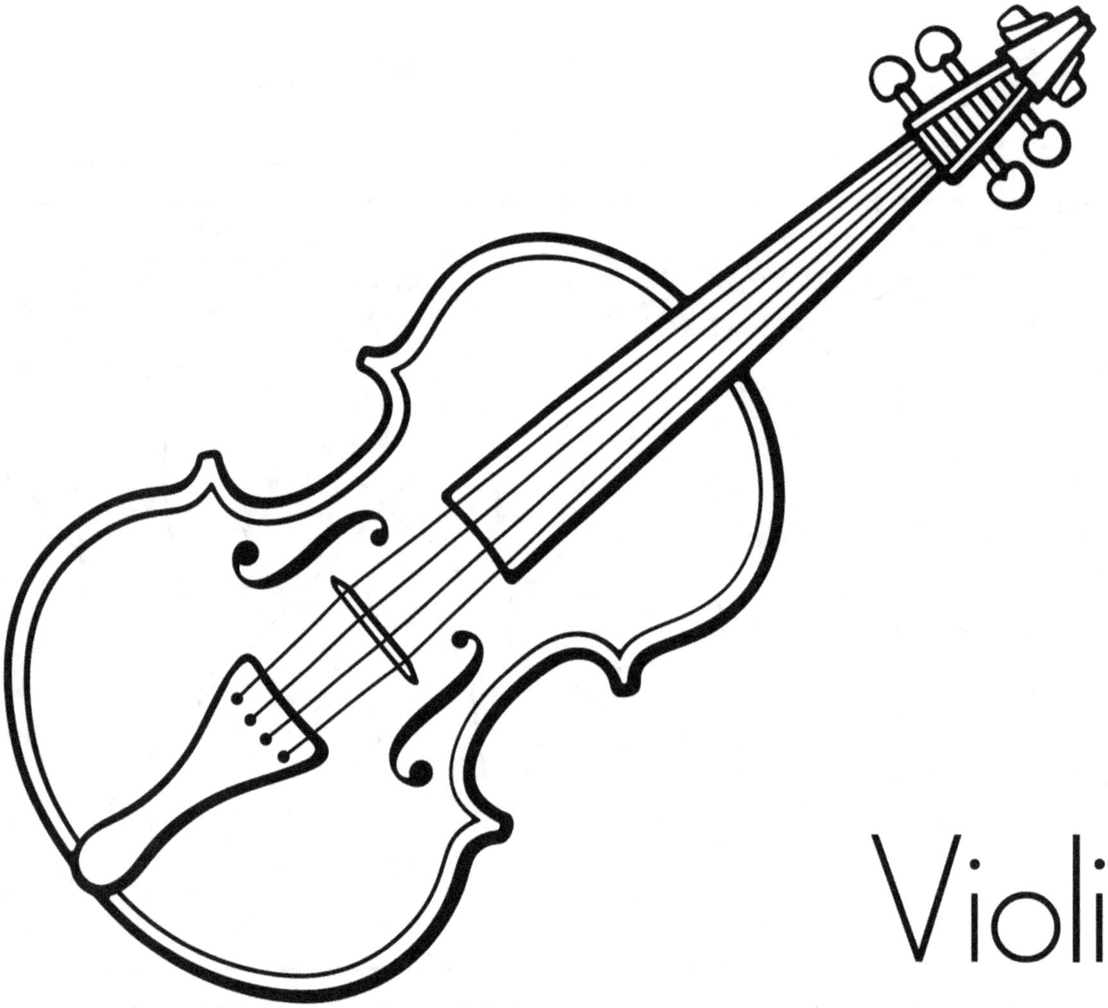

Violin

Practice writing the uppercase letter V.

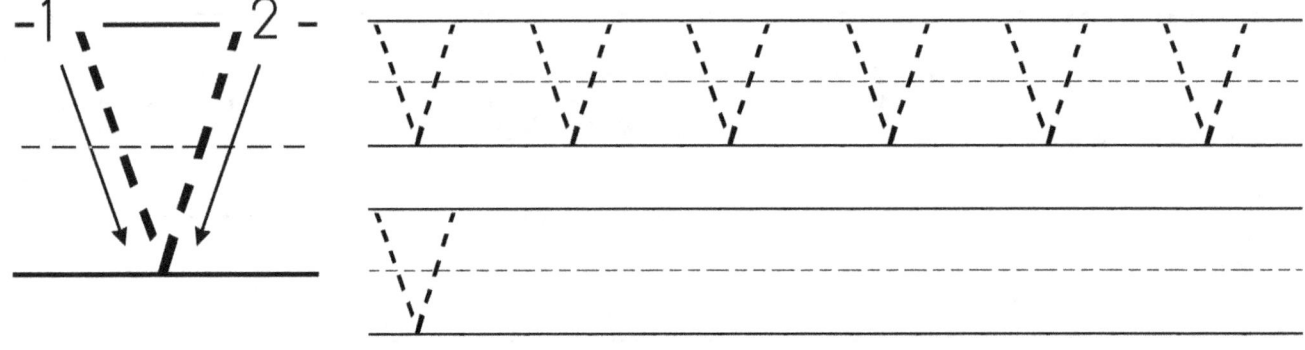

Color all the V letters.

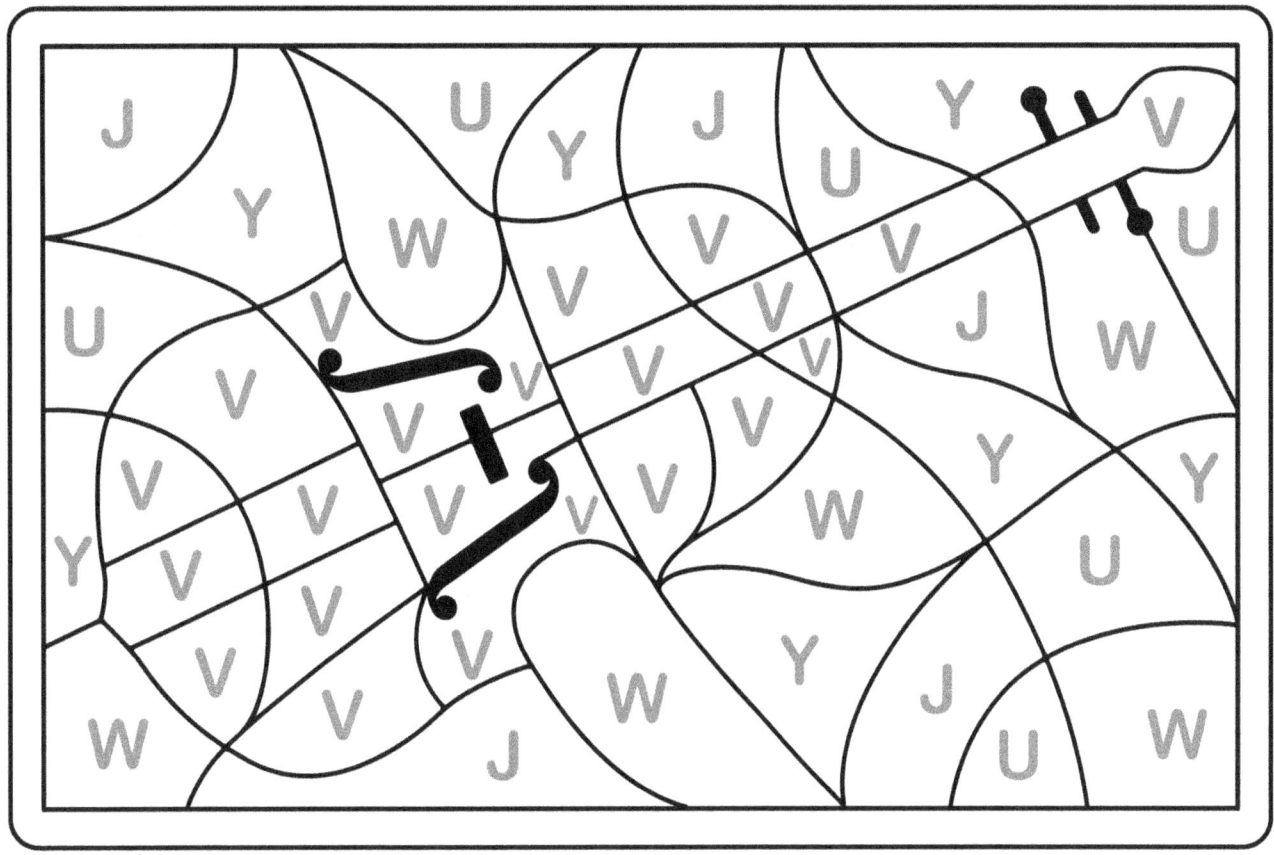

Practice writing the lowercase letter v.

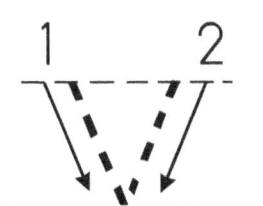
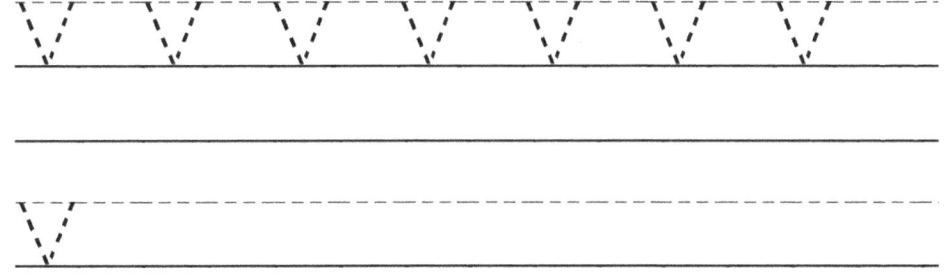

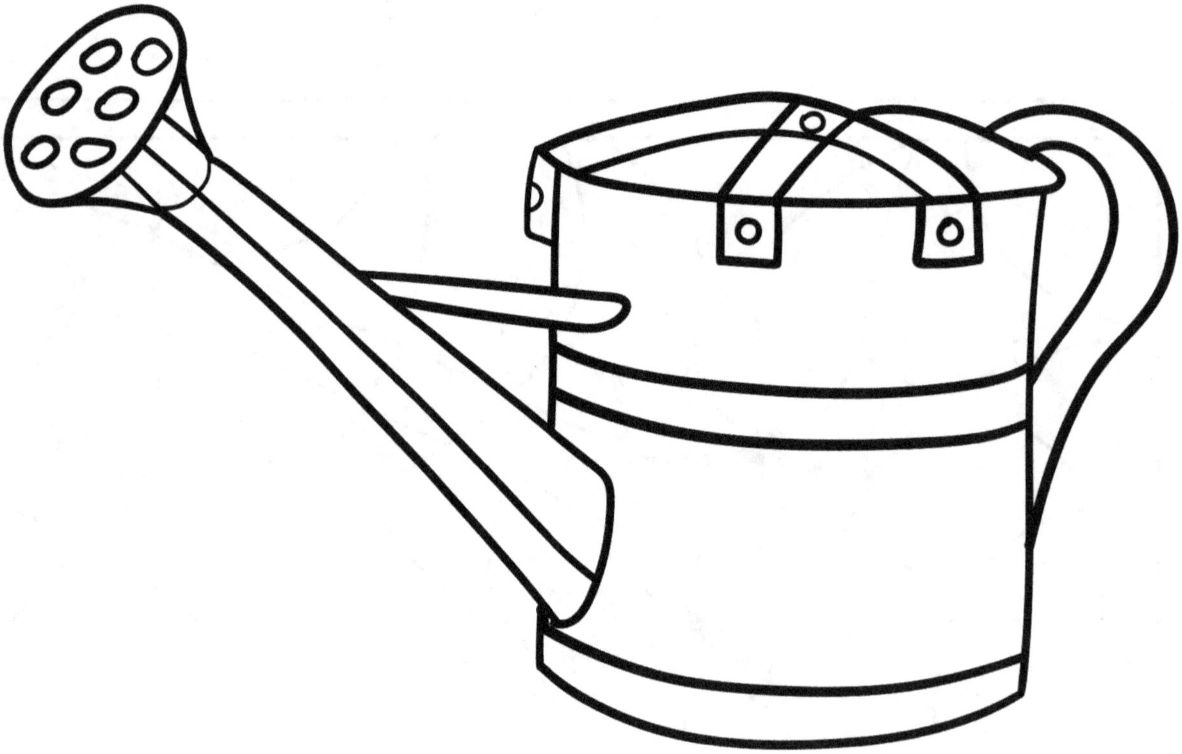

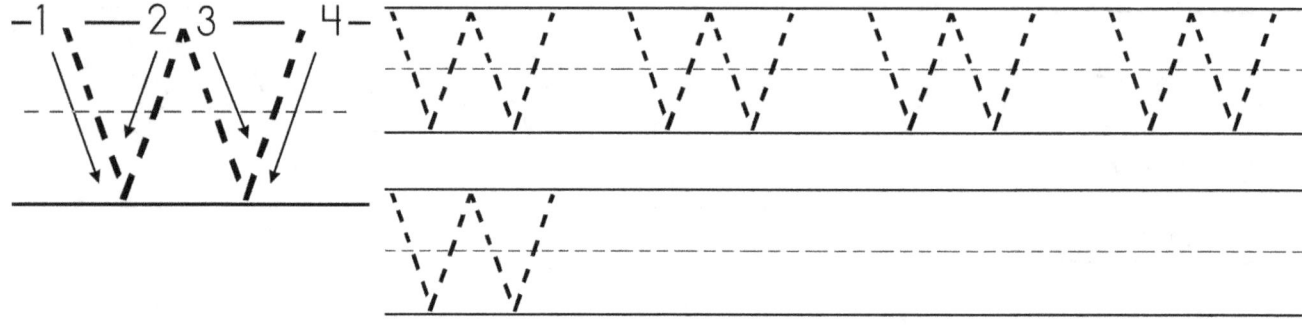

Watering can

Practice writing the uppercase letter W.

45

Color all the W letters.

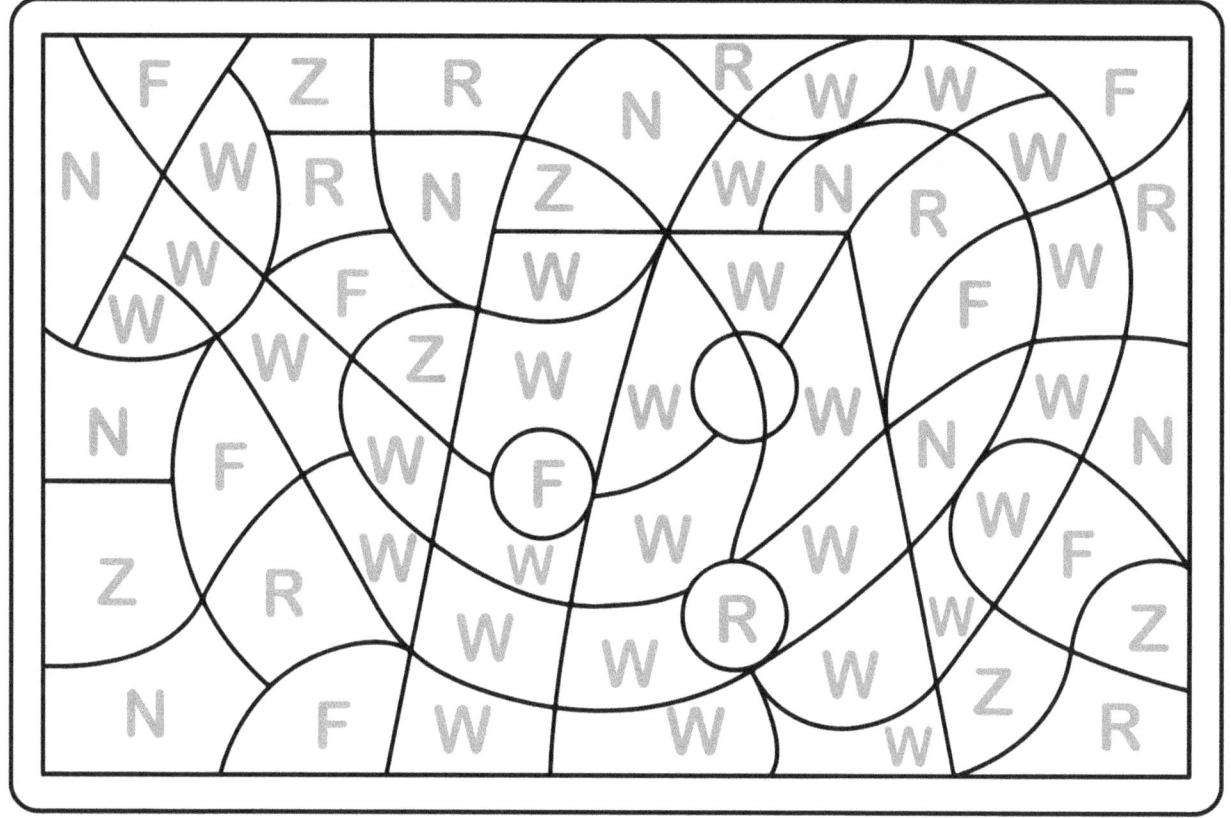

Practice writing the lowercase letter w.

Xx

X-Ray

Practice writing the uppercase letter X.

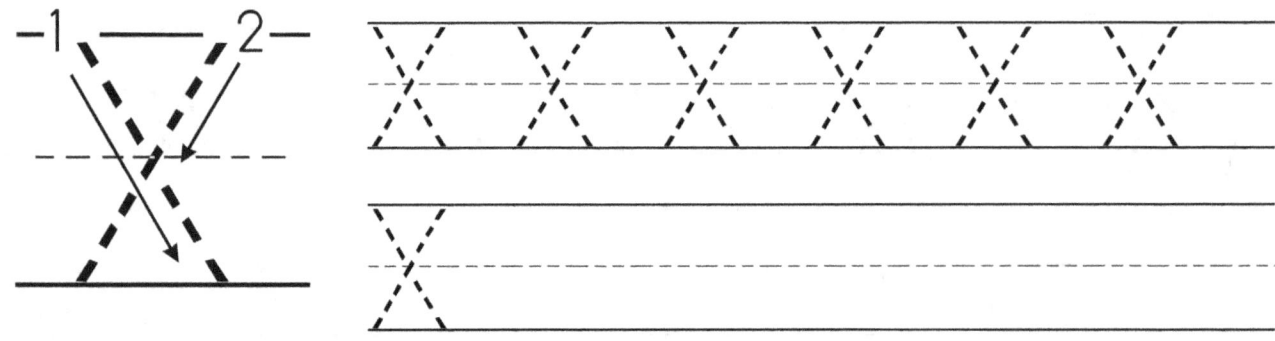

Color all the X letters.

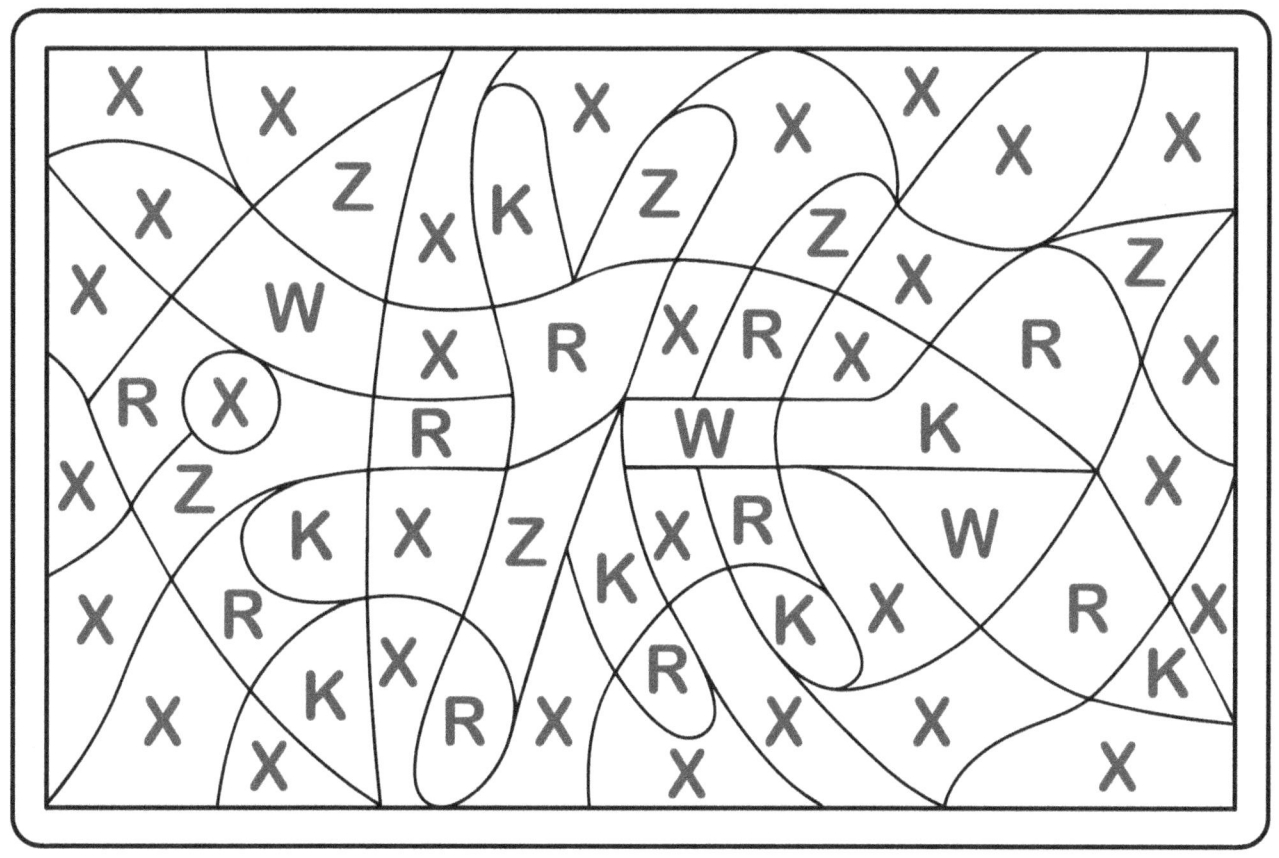

Practice writing the lowercase letter x.

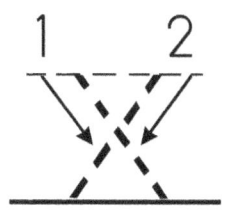
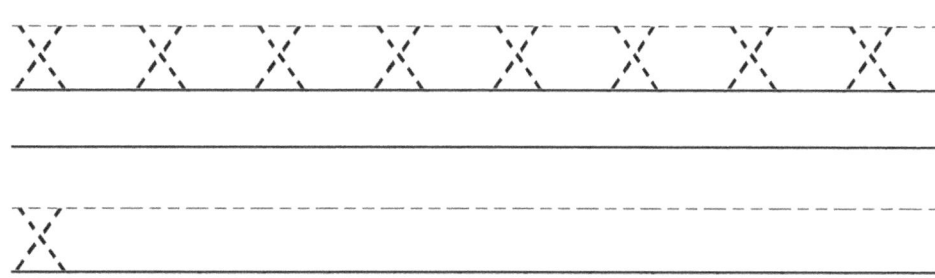

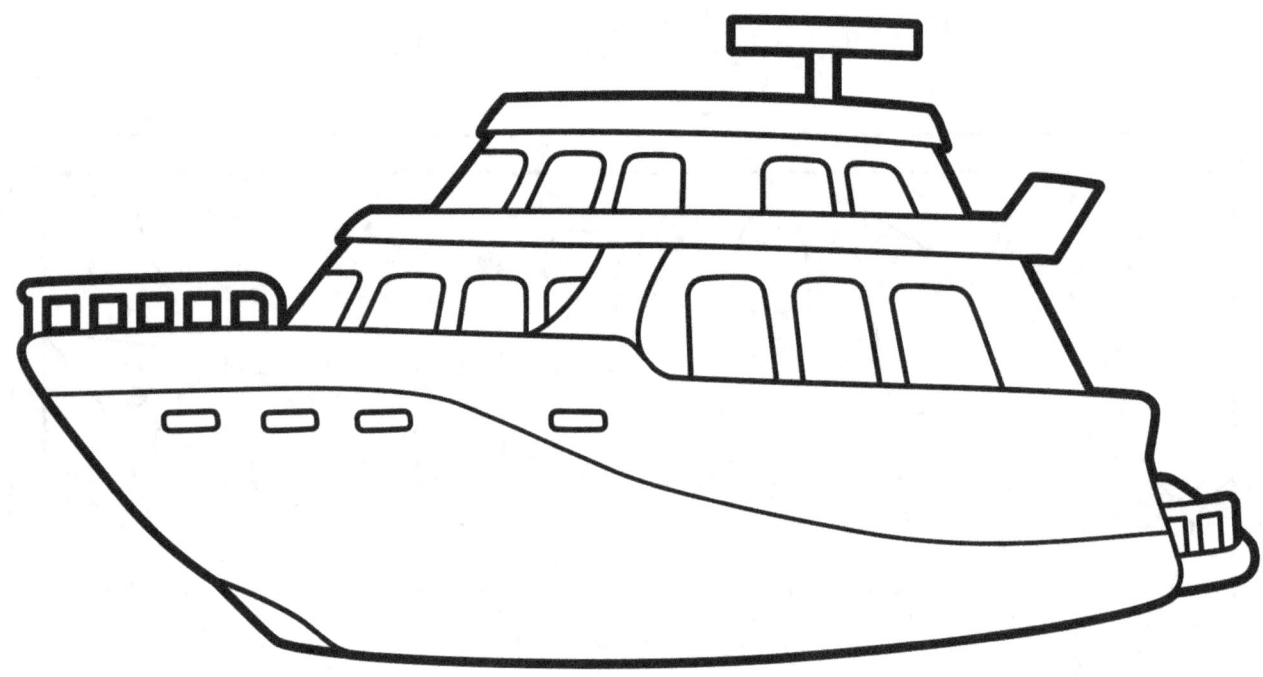

Yacht

Practice writing the uppercase letter Y.

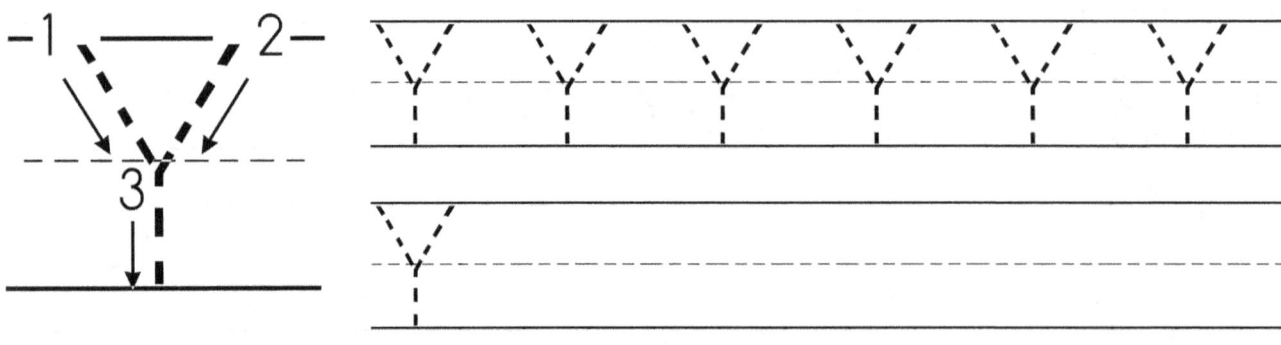

Color all the Y letters.

Practice writing the lowercase letter y.

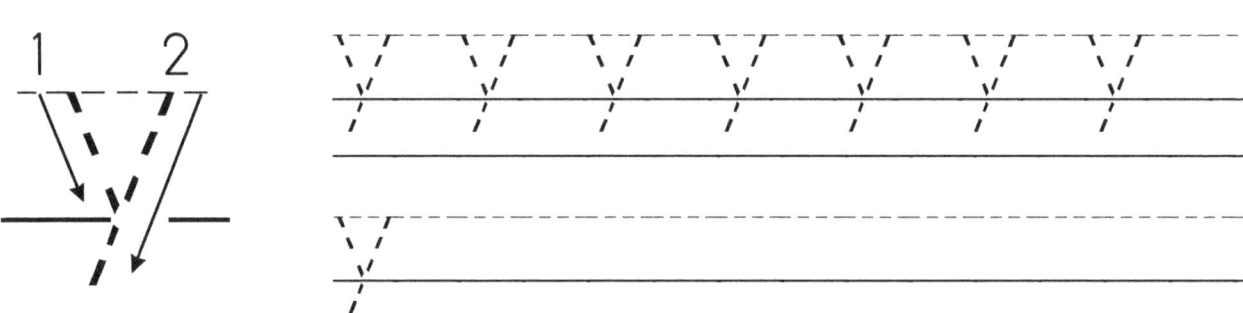

50

Zz

Zipper

Practice writing the uppercase letter Z.

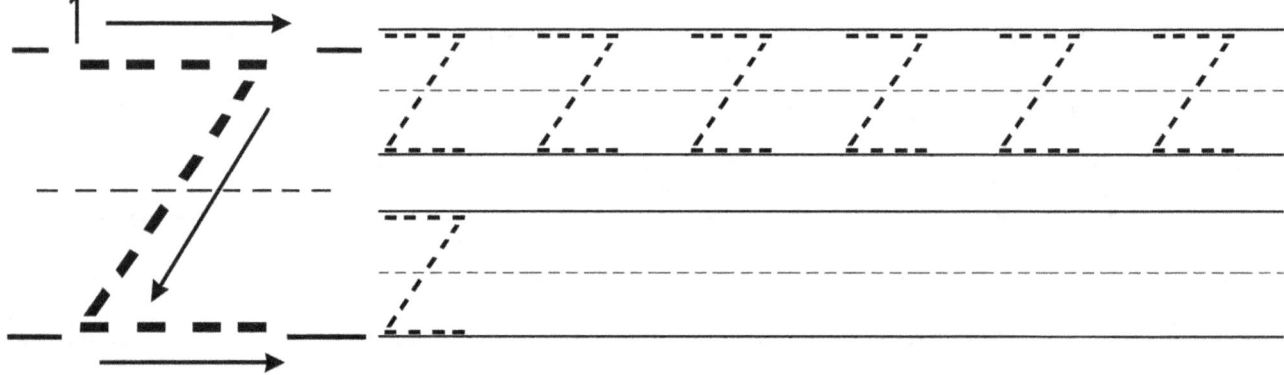

Zz

Color all the Z letters.

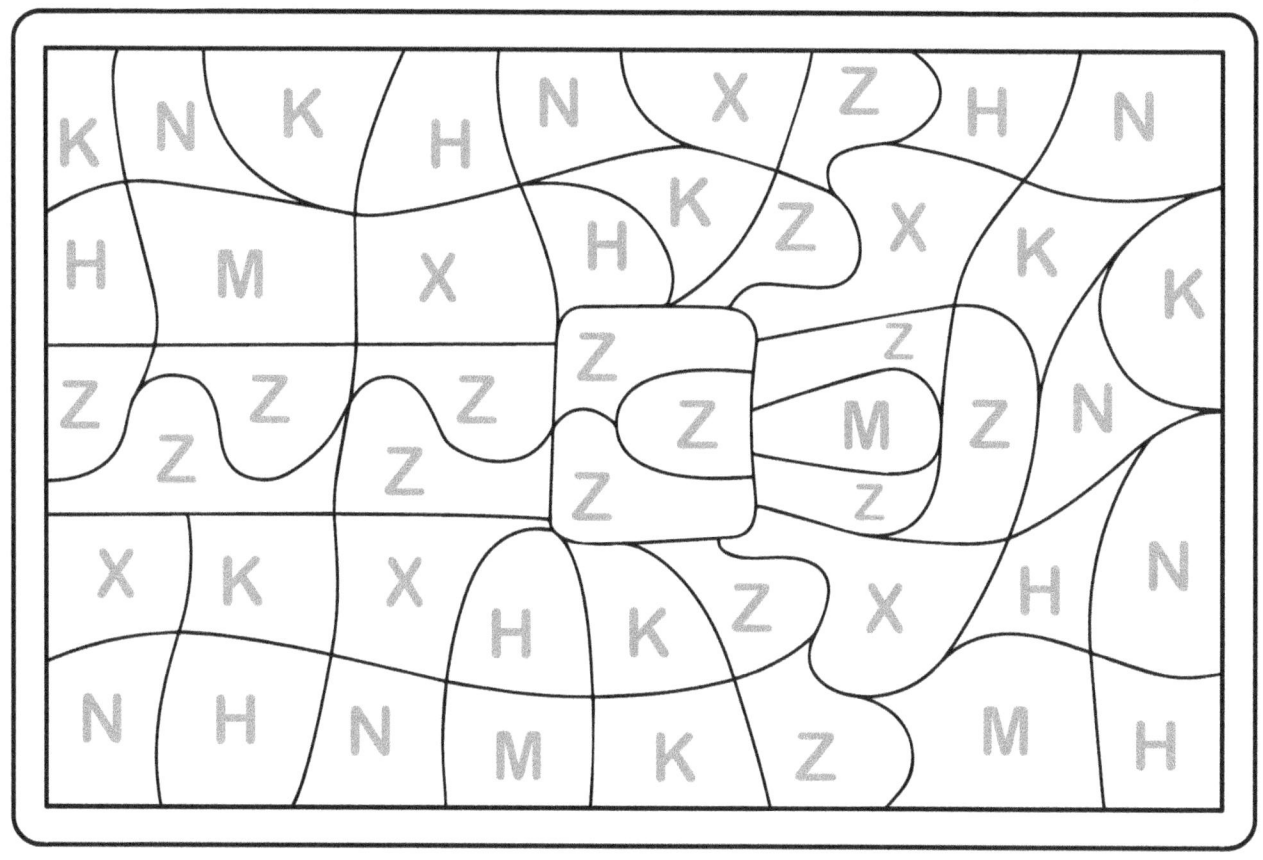

Practice writing the lowercase letter z.

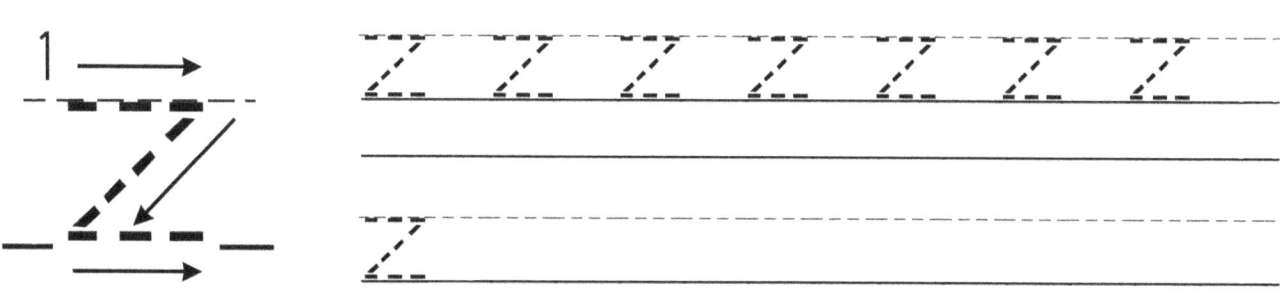

UPPERCASE HANDWRITING PRACTICE

A B C D E F G

H I J K L M

N O P Q R S T

U V W X Y Z

LOWERCASE HANDWRITING PRACTICE

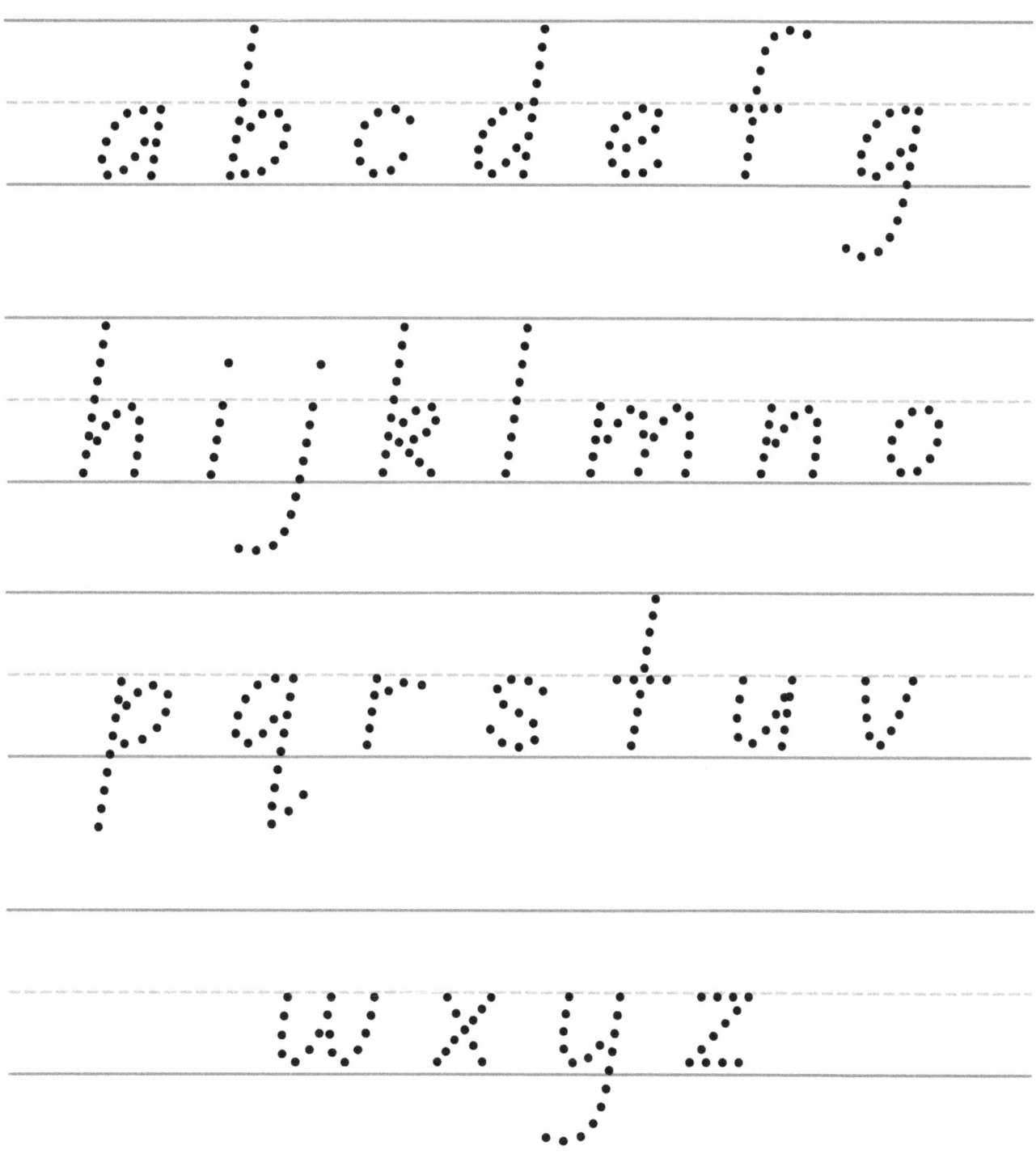

Let's Match Lowercase and Uppercase Letters

Draw line to match the lowercase and uppercase letters.
Color the matching puzzle pieces.

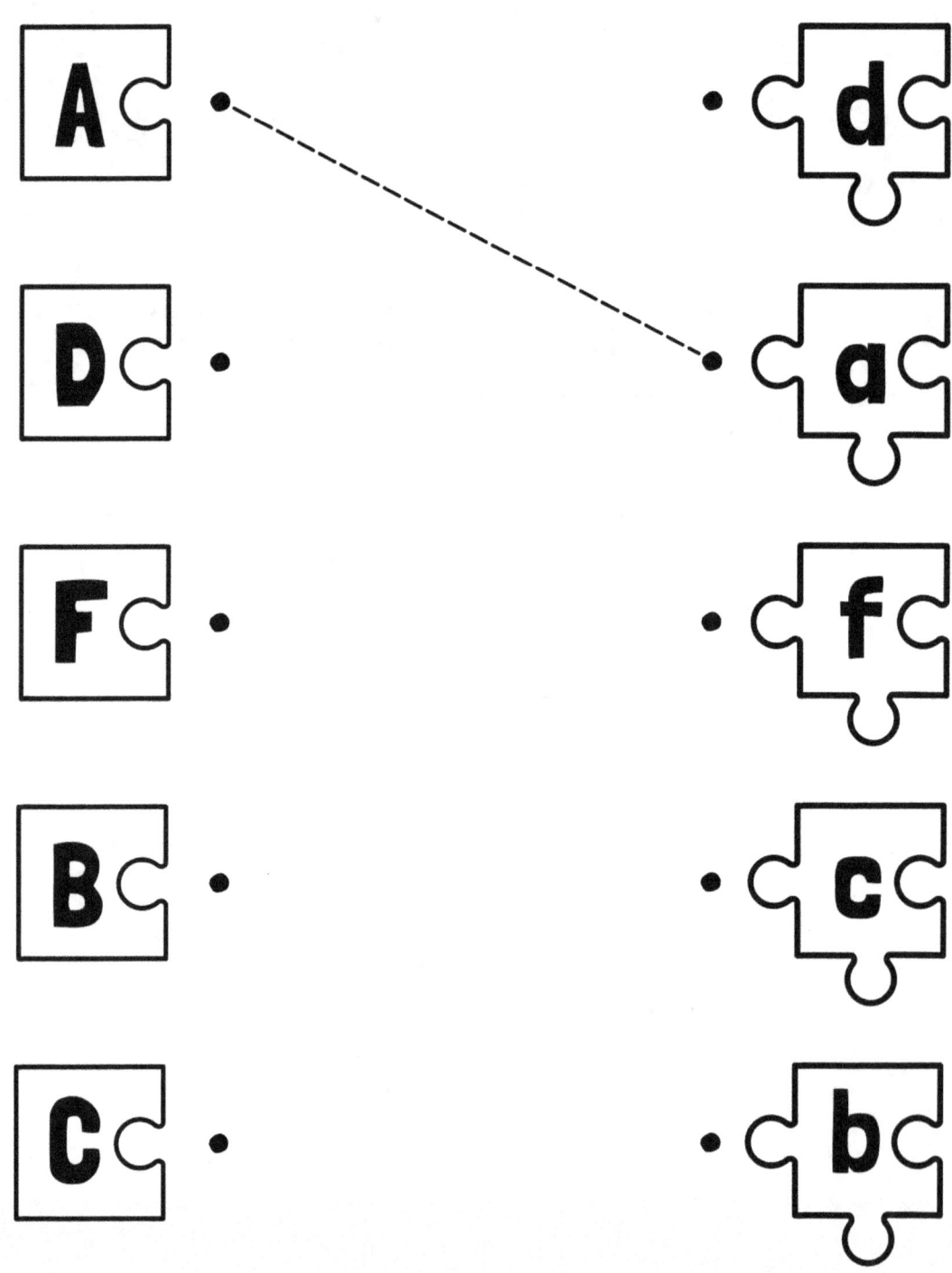

E · · p

M · · e

P · · m

O · · n

N · · r

R · · o

K •	• u
T •	• v
V •	• t
W •	• k
U •	• z
Z •	• w

Fill the missing letters

Help the ladybgu fill in the missing letters on his circle.

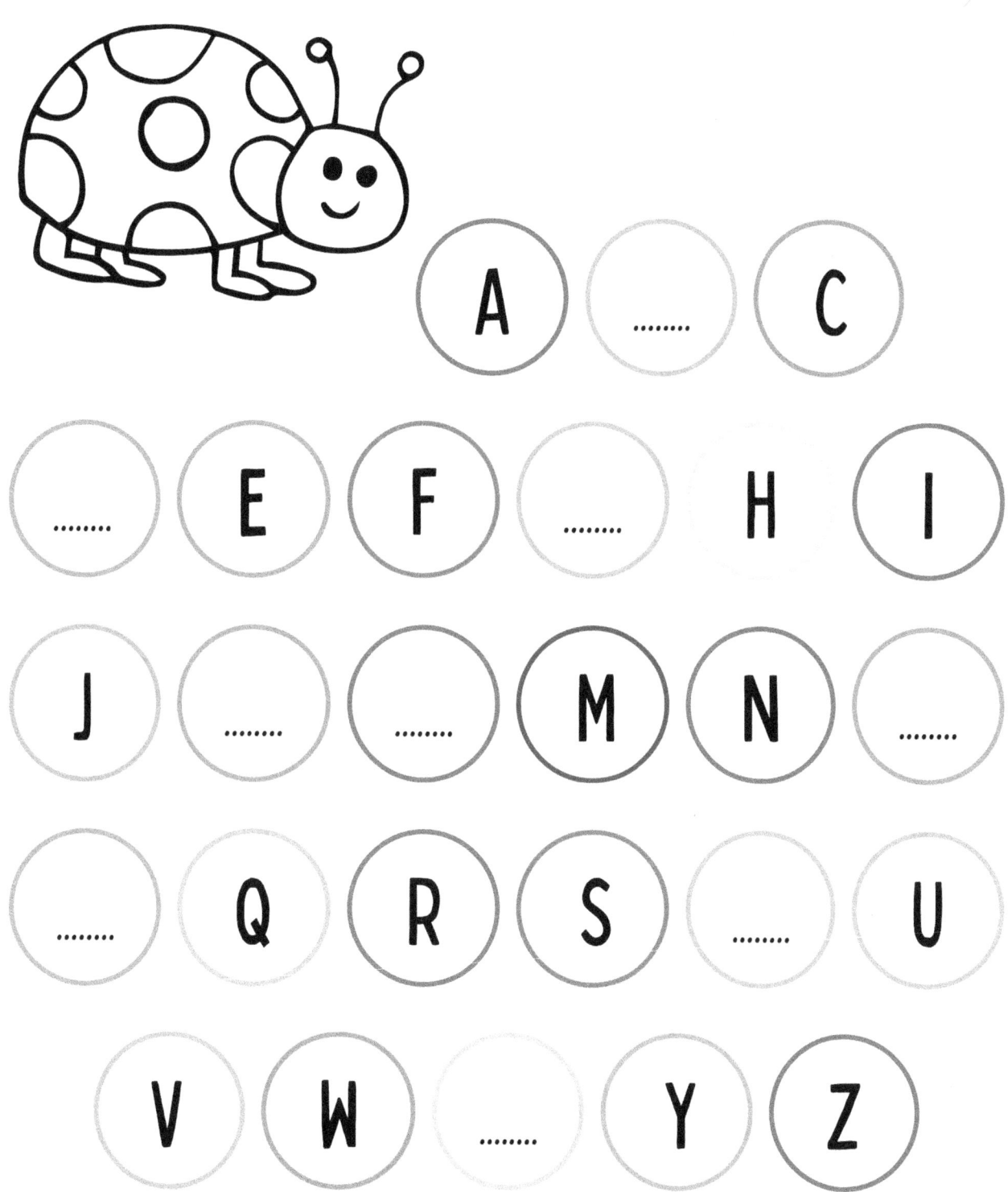

58

FILL IN THE MISSING BIG LETTERS

FILL IN THE MISSING BIG LETTERS

ABOUT THE AUTHOR

Mare Robbins is passionately committed to the development and education of children. As a mother to three kids herself, she firmly holds the view that it's never too premature to engage a child with the captivating world of books.

Her latest creation, an Alphabet Tracing and Color-by-Letter Workbook, offers your child an enjoyable and effortless way to master writing and penmanship. As your child engages with the workbook, they'll naturally develop essential skills such as hand-eye coordination, dexterity, and pen control.

Emphasizing the principle that practice fosters mastery, this workbook is designed to provide numerous opportunities for your child's learning and growth.

If you found this book beneficial, Mare would be deeply appreciative of a review on any platform where the book is available. Your kind words and encouragement serve as motivation for her to continue creating more enriching resources for children.

CERTIFICATE
of COMPLETION

Presented to

_____

For

_____

Date _____   Signed _____

www.ingramcontent.com/pod-product-compliance
Lightning Source LLC
Chambersburg PA
CBHW081158070526
44583CB00021B/2897